BARRIERS
TO TRADE
between
CANADA AND THE UNITED STATES

by

Francis Masson
and
J. B. Whitely

CANADIAN-AMERICAN COMMITTEE
Sponsored by
National Association (U.S.A.)
Private Planning Association of Canada

Reports on

Canada-United States Relations

WHEAT SURPLUSES AND THEIR IMPACT ON CANADA-UNITED STATES RELATIONS, by *W. E. Hamilton* and *W. M. Drummond*, xi and 52 pp., $1.00

OIL AND CANADA-UNITED STATES RELATIONS, by *John Davis*, xii and 36 pp., $1.00

NATURAL GAS AND CANADA-UNITED STATES RELATIONS, by *John Davis*, xii and 32 pp., $1.00

THE GROWTH OF SOVIET ECONOMIC POWER AND ITS CONSEQUENCES FOR CANADA AND THE UNITED STATES, by *Franklin A. Lindsay*, ix and 27 pp., $1.00

THE GROWTH AND CHANGING COMPOSITION OF TRADE BETWEEN CANADA AND THE UNITED STATES, by *Grant L. Reuber*, xii and 87 pp., $2.00

BARRIERS TO TRADE BETWEEN CANADA AND THE UNITED STATES, by *Francis Masson* and *J. B. Whitely*, xi and 97 pp., $2.00

For convenient library reference, the following
Library of Congress Card Catalogue Number
has been obtained: 60-11594
April 1960, $2.00

Quotation with appropriate credit
is permissible

National Planning Association and
Private Planning Association of Canada, 1960

Printed in Canada

 57

ii

Contents

Tables

Acknowledgment

The preparation of this study was made possible in part by funds granted by the Carnegie Corporation of New York. This foundation is not, however, author, owner, publisher, or proprietor of this publication, and is not to be understood as approving by virtue of its grants any of the statements made or views expressed therein.

The Canadian-American Committee

The Canadian-American Committee was established in 1957 to study problems arising from growing interdependence between Canada and the United States. With approximately equal representation from coast to coast in the two countries, its 60 members are business, labour, agricultural and professional leaders. The Committee is sponsored by two nonprofit research organizations—the National Planning Association in the United States and the Private Planning Association of Canada.

The Committee believes that good relations between Canada and the United States are essential for the future prosperity, and perhaps even the survival of both countries. It is therefore seeking not only to encourage a better understanding of the problems which have arisen and may arise, but also to develop solutions for such problems which are in the common interest of both countries. The Committee is taking a North American approach in its search for constructive programs.

The Committee is sponsoring a series of objective research studies on various aspects of Canadian-American relations. These are being undertaken by qualified experts in both countries and, with the Committee's approval, will be published. On the basis of these factual studies and of discussions at its meetings, the Committee also issues policy statements signed by its members. Such statements are directed at increasing public understanding of the attitudes, policies and actions which the Committee believes would best serve the mutual interests of the peoples of both countries.

The Canadian-American Committee is a unique organization, both in terms of its broadly diversified membership, and in terms of its blending of factual studies and policy conclusions on Canadian-American relations. It meets twice a year, once in Canada and once in the United States. Its work is jointly financed by funds contributed from private sources in the United States and Canada, and by foundation grants.

Offices on behalf of the Committee are maintained at 1606 New Hampshire Avenue, N. W., Washington 9, D.C. and at 716 Sun Life Building, Montreal, Quebec. John Miller (Assistant Chairman and Executive Secretary of N.P.A.) serves as Secretary of the Committee, and Arthur J. R. Smith (Secretary of P.P.A.C.) is Director of Research.

R. Douglas Stuart

Robert M. Fowler

Co-chairmen of the Committee

Statement

by the Canadian-American Committee on "Barriers to Trade between Canada and the United States"

Despite the commanding importance to both Canada and the United States of their transborder economic ties, the economies of the two countries are partially insulated from each other by government restrictions and controls on international trade. The impact of these barriers to trade varies greatly as among different areas of economic activity—producers of certain agricultural commodities are strongly affected, while trade in forest products and minerals is typically affected only slightly or not at all. In the field of secondary manufactures, both countries deliberately use trade barriers as a means of limiting imports and promoting domestic production.

There has been considerable discussion in recent years about various aspects of commercial trade barriers between Canada and the United States, particularly in the context of their adverse effects on the development of a more highly integrated and specialized structure of industry in North America. But there does not appear to be any brief published description of the existing framework of such obstacles—tariffs, tariff administration, import controls and quotas, and other non-tariff obstacles. The Committee has sponsored this study with the aim of contributing not only to a broader public understanding of the facts about existing trade barriers, but also to the development of useful background material for other studies of trade and commercial policy.

The introductory chapter of this report relates the pattern of Canadian and U.S. trade barriers to the current flow of transborder trade. However, although the report does indicate the restrictiveness of trade barriers on a large number of individual products, it emphasizes that in the field of secondary manufacture in particular, only intensive analysis on a case-by-case basis can fully explain the consequences of these barriers.

The following four chapters present in broad outline the nature of the considerable volume of trade which does move freely across the border, the system of tariffs and quotas of Canada and of the United States, and the pervasive set of administrative controls which comprise an additional "invisible" set of barriers to trade. Chapters 6 and 7 examine the impact of trade barriers on selected agricultural and industrial commodities and on manufactured products.

This snap-shot picture of present trade barriers does not provide a detailed historical analysis of the development of commercial policy—of which tariffs are the principal component—by Canada and the United States. Neither does it examine the effects, over time, of past changes in tariffs and other trade barriers upon the composition of trade between the two countries or the growth and development of industry, mining and agriculture.

Other studies are being undertaken by the Committee to place these matters in historical perspective. The present work is limited to assembling the relevant facts about current barriers to trade. In due course, after the completion of other descriptive and analytic reports about Canadian and U.S. trade, the Committee itself expects to develop recommendations relating to Canadian-American trade problems.

This report was prepared by Dr. Francis Masson, of the Committee staff, and Mr. J. B. Whitely, with the advice and active collaboration of a large number of Canadian and American experts in this field.

Members of the Canadian-American Committee Signing the Statement

Co-chairmen of the Committee

ROBERT M. FOWLER
President
Canadian Pulp & Paper Association

R. DOUGLAS STUART
Chairman of the Board
The Quaker Oats Company

Members

ARTHUR S. ADAMS
President, American Council on Education

WILLIAM L. BATT
Philadelphia, Penna.

RALPH P. BELL
Vice-President, Bank of Nova Scotia

L. J. BELNAP
Chairman, Consolidated Paper Corporation Limited

HAROLD BOESCHENSTEIN
President, Owens-Corning Fiberglas Corporation

J. E. BROWNLEE
President, United Grain Growers Limited

L. S. BUCKMASTER
General President, United Rubber, Cork, Linoleum and Plastic Workers of America, AFL-CIO

GEORGE BURT
Director, Region No. 7, United Automobile, Aircraft & Agricultural Implement Workers of America, AFL-CIO-CLC

BROOKE CLAXTON
Vice-President and General Manager, Metropolitan Life Insurance Company

A. HOLLIS EDENS
President, Duke University

MARCEL FARIBAULT
President and General Manager, General Trust of Canada

HAROLD S. FOLEY
Vice-Chairman of the Board, MacMillan, Bloedel and Powell River Limited

CLINTON S. GOLDEN
Solebury, Bucks County, Penna.

DONALD GORDON
Chairman and President, Canadian National Railways

W. L. GORDON
President, J. D. Woods & Gordon Limited

H. H. HANNAM
President, Canadian Federation of Agriculture

F. PEAVEY HEFFELFINGER
Chairman of the Board, F. H. Peavey & Company

JAMES H. HILTON
President, Iowa State College

STANLEY C. HOPE
President, SoundScriber Corporation

T. V. HOUSER
Director Sears, Roebuck & Co.

CHARLES L. HUSTON, JR.
President, Lukens Steel Company

CLAUDE JODOIN
President, Canadian Labour Congress

J. H. MOWBRAY JONES
President, Bowaters Mersey Paper Co. Ltd.

JOSEPH D. KEENAN
International Secretary, International Brotherhood of Electrical Workers, AFL-CIO

R. A. LAIDLAW
Secretary and Director, R. Laidlaw Lumber Company Limited

MAURICE LAMONTAGNE
Ottawa, Ontario

E. H. LANE
Chairman and Director, The Lane Company, Inc.

HERBERT H. LANK
President, DuPont Company of Canada Limited

DONALD MacDONALD
Secretary-Treasurer, Canadian Labour Congress

W. A. MACKINTOSH
Vice-Chancellor and Principal, Queen's University

1

Introduction

The Setting

THIS STUDY attempts to summarize in as brief a compass as possible the barriers to trade between Canada and the United States, and to provide some assessment of the restrictiveness of present levels of protection. One of the most striking features of the analysis is the variety and complexity of the methods used by each country to keep out the other's goods. Tariffs are probably the principal barriers, but few people in either country appreciate the extent to which the tariffs of each country have been supplemented by other forms of protection. Indeed, for some industries, quantitative restrictions have had a much more severe impact on the flow of trade than tariffs.

In the realm of non-tariff barriers are also found such devices as special provisions for valuation and classification and delays in administering the regulations, which raise additional effective barriers and may not only make it difficult for an importer especially in the United States to find out in advance the rate or amount of duty he will be called upon to pay, but may also provide means by which traders can be harassed by domestic producers. Uncertainty has an economic price. Other devices include marking regulations, copyright, patent and trade-mark provisions, and food, drug and health regulations. The purchasing by either government usually discriminates against the goods of the other country. Both countries tend to use administrative devices to supplement the straightforward protection provided by the tariff, and that these devices constitute a significant barrier to trade between the two countries. At the same time, at least some progress has been made in the past two or three years to remove some of the uncertainty and clarify the rates.

In trying to appraise the degree to which tariffs themselves are a barrier, there does not appear to be much statistical evidence for drawing general conclusions. Attempts to use ratios of duty paid to value of imports founder on the fact that high tariff rates tend to exclude imports. The calculation is clearly biased in a downward direction. The over-all averaging of tariff rates not only suffers from the extreme complexity of tariff schedules, with their mixed ad valorem (percent of value) and specific duties, but it gives equal weight to important and unimportant items. If some kind of generalization can be made, however, it would include the following points.

Both Canadian and U.S. tariffs are relatively low on primary materials and higher on manufactured goods. The tariff structures of both countries have, in fact, developed around the fundamental principle that the entry of raw materials for industry should be made much easier than the entry of more finished products which that industry produces. It is suggested that on manufactured goods most U.S. and Canadian tariffs lie in a range of 10 to 25 percent, but with the dispersion both above and below this range tending to be more pronounced for U.S. tariffs.

In looking at the possible effects of these restrictions on the flow of trade, one must begin with the fact that the volume of trade is very great. It is a commonplace that each country is the other's best customer. Total trade across the border is now about seven billion dollars per year. The level of economic advancement of the two countries, the economic advantages to be derived from the exchange of products, the similarity of the two peoples in temperament and interests, all provide a natural basis for a large volume of trade. Yet it is difficult not to be persuaded that the total could be much greater were there no restrictions. It is by looking more deeply into the trade figures that the effects of tariff rates and other forms of protection begin to appear.

Fully three-quarters of Canadian exports to the United States are concentrated in a few groups: agricultural products, metals and minerals, lumber products, pulp and newsprint. On these products, the U.S. tariff is low, and many of the products have free entry. Even in the manufactured goods category, U.S. imports tend to be concentrated in a few industrial groups, notably agricultural machinery (which is permitted free entry both ways across the border) and alcoholic beverages. The Canadian picture is considerably different. At least three-quarters of Canadian imports from the United States are manufactured goods. Unless these goods are exempted from duty because of special "end-use" provisions, most appear to come in over tariffs that range between 10 and 25 percent, and perhaps average about 15 percent. Some of these goods nevertheless compete effectively with those of Canadian producers, and hold a very substantial proportion of the Canadian market.

In summary, the U.S. tariff has much the effect on U.S. imports as one would expect from a tariff structure designed to favor the domestic production of manufactured goods. It is, in fact, argued by many Canadian economic historians that the structure of the U.S. tariff has simultaneously been as responsible as the Canadian tariff for shaping the development of Canadian industry. The Canadian tariff's main role has been to permit manufacturing of a reasonably economic nature to develop in Canada, with a substantial volume of imports preventing Canadian costs from straying too far from U.S. levels.

It seems fairly clear that any assessment of the relative "levels" of tariff protection must take this last factor into account. Even if Canadian tariffs on manufactured goods are higher than American—and they do look somewhat higher—the over-all pattern of trade does not support the conclusion that they are more restrictive. Although U.S. manufacturers have a substantial share of the Canadian market, the Canadian share of the U.S. market is infinitesimal. Moreover, the balance of trade and payments has been consistently in the favour of the United States, with the Canadian current account deficit now running over $1,500 million, of which about three-quarters arises from merchandise transactions.

Both Canadian and U.S. secondary manufacturing industries have been developed primarily to serve the domestic markets. Since the U.S. market is some 15 to 20 times as large as the Canadian market, U.S. manufacturers can obtain much greater economies of scale (larger production runs, more specialization in machinery and labour, and lower costs of overhead and distribution). Largely as a result of this one factor, the average cost of manufacturing in Canada, excluding such primary industries as pulp and newsprint where scale is no problem, run some 35 to 40 percent higher than in the United States. Although lower wages in Canada provide some offset to this productivity differential, it is easy to appreciate why the volume of manufactured imports from the United States is so great in spite of the Canadian tariff.

Some parts of the following analysis implicitly raise the problem posed by this cost differential on the prospects for larger exports of Canadian manufactured goods to the United States. There appears to be no simple answer to this question. There are wide differences between industries, and it is only by detailed industry studies that conclusions of substance could be reached. However, in spite of the average differential in costs, a respectable proportion of Canadian industry might become competitive with that of the United States, given easier access to U.S. markets on a long-run basis.

The Scope and Nature of This Study

At the outset, it should be emphasized that this study does not purport to be a comprehensive description and appraisal of Canadian-American trade trends, trade problems and commercial policy. The limited objective is to present a snap-shot picture of present barriers to trade between the two countries. Thus, the study presents no detailed analysis of the growth and changing composition of transborder trade; nor does it discuss changes in

3

trade barriers in the past. These subjects are specifically examined in companion reports.[1]

Within this deliberately confined area, the following chapters outline the segments of free transborder trade, the structure of existing tariffs and quotas, the so-called invisible barriers which are broadly termed "administrative protectionism" and groups of commodities subject to barriers of various degrees of restrictiveness.

It is clear that although a very substantial proportion of total transborder trade moves virtually unhindered between Canada and the United States, this trade is heavily concentrated among a relatively few products—for example, newsprint, pulpwood, wood pulp, iron ore, uranium, asbestos, and agricultural machinery from Canada to the United States; and certain automobile parts, farm equipment, drilling apparatus, iron ore, anthracite coal, aircraft, oranges, and soya beans from the United States to Canada.

Considering the diversity and number of products which flow across the border subject to barriers of some kind, and considering not only the wide variations in tariff rates but also the different structures of barriers in Canada and the United States (as well as the costs of uncertainty), it is impossible to reach any clear-cut conclusion as to whether Canadian or U.S. barriers are more restrictive. No such general conclusion is ventured in this study. But having regard to various appropriate factors from case to case, some tentative findings have been advanced regarding the restrictiveness of barriers against a number of particular commodities.

In the case of agricultural products, for example, the U.S. barriers affect such Canadian commodities as wheat, potatoes, and flaxseed and linseed oil, while the Canadian barriers affect some types of U.S. vegetables and non-citrus fruits, turkeys and some dairy products.

In the case of raw materials, both countries have generally low barriers or none at all. There are a few items, however, especially on the U.S. side, which are subject to restrictive quotas or tariffs—for example, lead and zinc, fluorspar and barite. Some raw materials produced in Canada are given moderate protection. Among primary manufactures, many barriers are restrictive on both sides, and frequently for the same products—for example, in the case of primary textiles, a number of primary metal products such as copper wire and tubing, and various primary chemical, paper, and other products.

It is in the field of secondary manufactures that the restrictiveness of existing barriers is most difficult to appraise, especially in the case of capital-

---

1. See "The Growth and Changing Composition of Trade between Canada and the United States" by Grant L. Reuber, published on behalf of the Canadian-American Committee, by the Private Planning Association of Canada and the National Planning Association, U.S.A., 1960. See also the forthcoming report for by the Committee by Constant Southworth and W. W. Buchanan on changes in trade barriers between Canada and the United States over the past quarter century.

intensive, high-productivity industries. While the study does single out a few specific illustrations of restrictive barriers for individual products—for example, some chemical products, finished textiles and some types of industrial machinery—it is emphasized that only further intensive study on a case-by-case basis can provide sound and objective indications of the restrictiveness of these barriers. It is obvious, however, that both countries have used trade barriers as a deliberate and effective device for encouraging domestic manufacturing and limiting imports, and that it is especially in this field that "administrative protectionism" has been used to augment the tariff obstacles. This has had the important result of blocking a more highly integrated and specialized development of industry in Canada and the United States.

Finally, the study reveals a number of salient similarities and differences between the structure and administration of trade obstacles between Canada and the United States. Among the similarities are such things as: the typical progression of tariff rates from zero or low figures on raw materials to much higher rates on secondary manufactures; the use of effective barriers on scattered agricultural products in both countries; and broadly similar valuation provisions and certain other features of administering tariffs. Among the major differences are: the relatively much heavier reliance on legislative and judicial procedures in the United States, as compared with the reliance on administrative procedures in Canada. In part, of course, this relates to differences in the structure of tariffs—such as the differentials in Canadian tariffs as between classes of items made in Canada and those not made in Canada. But this difference carries all the way through to such matters as appeals against classification and valuation decisions. In the United States, the ultimate recourse, except on matters of law, is the Customs Court; in Canada, it is through the Department of National Revenue to the Tariff Board (only strict matters of law can be brought before the Exchequer Court).

Beyond such broad differences are myriads of detailed differences. It is only by viewing these differences in detail that one can get any true perspective on the enormous complexities of the structure of barriers and the complications arising in their administration.

2

The Area of Free Trade

Free Lists and Free Items

THE TARIFF SCHEDULES of both Canada and the United States specify that certain items shall enter duty-free. The U.S. free list (see Chapter 3) applies indiscriminately to imports from all countries. The principal Canadian exports to the United States falling under the free list are newsprint, wood pulp, iron ore, agricultural implements, asbestos, pulp wood and abrasives.

Canada also provides for free entry of many items. Some articles are allowed free entry under both the British Preferential and the Most-Favored-Nation columns; others under the British Preferential column only. In some cases, such as agricultural machinery, all articles of a particular kind enter duty-free, but in others there are certain qualifications. For example, many articles, such as automobile ball bearings, are free only if they are "of a class or kind not made in Canada"; otherwise, duty is charged. In other instances, an article is only allowed free entry if it is to be used for a particular purpose in Canada—an example is cotton yarn "when imported by manufacturers for use exclusively in the manufacture of levers' lace in their own factories".

Certain items are charged duty by Canada at the border, but a large portion of the duty is later remitted to the importer. In most cases, such as tariff item 1052—"machinery of a class or kind not made in Canada" when used in the plants of automobile manufacturers—a "drawback" of 99 percent is given, making the imported article virtually duty-free. Sometimes, however, some of the duty collected is remitted, as in the case of pipe used for construction of the Interprovincial, Trans-Mountain, Westcoast Transmission and Trans-Canada pipelines.

On the U.S. free list, there are 110 specific items for which there were imports of $100,000 or more from Canada in 1957. In contrast, there are over 500 no-duty items in the Canadian tariff lists for which there were imports of $100,000 from the United States in 1957. Major U.S. duty-free exports to Canada include such items as timber and planks, metallic ores, scrap iron, raw cotton, crude petroleum, synthetic resins, text and reference books, magazines and newspapers, and wire for use in the manufacture of barbed wire.

Examination of the rather heterogeneous list of duty-free items which cross the border in both directions reveals that a few are not directly competitive with home output—for example, nickel ore and matte, nickel oxide, asbestos, and antiques on the U.S. free list. However, the majority are items which appear to compete to some extent with home industry.

Technological progress has created new pressures from time to time, with the result that duty-free status has been accorded to some new items or revoked on others. The general tendency in both the United States and Canada over the past 30 years has been for the free items to decline both in number and in relative importance. Between 1929 and 1931, duty-free U.S. imports from Canada averaged about four-fifths of total imports as compared to only three-fifths today. A similar shrinking of the relative importance of free items among U.S. exports to Canada is observable, although the drop is less marked. The fact that the U.S. Tariff Act has not been revised in almost 30 years doubtless accounts for the persistence of some items, such as bread, which has recently begun to offer strong competition to some domestic producers near the Canadian border.

Duty-free U.S. Imports from Canada

Tables 1 and 2 give an over-all picture of the area of free trade between Canada and the United States. On the U.S. side, the salient feature is that nearly half of the duty-free goods imported from Canada consist of newsprint pulpwood and wood pulp. Duty-free wood products also include logs, poles, staves, railroad ties, laths, shakes, shingles, pickets, palings, and Christmas trees. Almost four-fifths of imports of forest products enter free of duty.

Almost half of the metallic minerals and metals group appears in the free column, due to free trade in iron, titanium, nickel, uranium and other metallic ores and concentrates, as well as refined cobalt, platinum and minor metals, and scrap of aluminum, brass, tin plate and magnesium. Free-list non-metallic minerals are mainly industrial diamonds, asbestos, abrasives, plaster rock and gypsum, which comprise about two-fifths of imports from Canada of this type.

The high concentration of duty-free items in the machinery and vehicles group is accounted for mainly by agricultural machinery and parts, which are marketed on a continental basis by large and efficient Canadian plants. This special case suggests the advantages which may be derived by Canadian manufacturers having easy access to U.S. markets. Canadian fertilizer plants also are every bit as efficient as their U.S. counterparts. A variety of other chemical products enter duty-free, such as creosote oil, benzene, napthalene

7

and coal tar distillates, sodium sulphate and sodium cyanamide, and hydrochloric and sulphuric acid. Additional free-list items include: hides, skins and furs; lobsters; fish meal and scraps; and slaughterhouse by-products.

TABLE 1

U.S. Duty-Free Imports from Canada, by Commodity Groups, Year Ending June 30, 1957

Commodity Group	Duty-free Imports	Total Imports	Free as a Percent of Total
	(Millions of Dollars)		
Wood and paper..........................	973.9	1,254.3	78
Metals and manufactures, except machinery and vehicles................	377.0	714.2	53
Non-metallic minerals	108.3	278.5	39
Miscellaneous...........................	95.8	107.5	89
Machinery and vehicles..................	95.3	136.9	70
Chemicals and related products...........	55.3	85.0	65
Animals and animal products, inedible......	34.7	45.8	76
Animals and animal products, edible........	21.4	119.1	18
Vegetable food products and beverages......	13.5	174.5	8
Textile fibers and manufactures...........	6.2	10.1	6
Vegetable products, inedible, except fibers and wood......................	2.9	16.2	18
Adjustments[1]...........................	5.1	35.0	—
Totals.................................	1,789.4	2,977.1	60

1. Shipments individually valued at $250 or less not classified.
Sources: U.S. Bureau of Customs; U.S. Bureau of the Census.

TABLE 2

Canadian Duty-Free Imports from the United States, by Commodity Groups, 1957

Commodity Group	Duty-free Imports	Total Imports	Free as a Percent of Total
	(Millions of Dollars)		
Iron and its products[1]	637.1	1,802.0	35
Miscellaneous...........................	262.5	417.7	63
Non-metallic minerals....................	171.1	391.3	44
Chemical and allied products.............	109.9	253.0	43
Wood, wood products and paper..........	99.7	201.2	50
Agricultural and vegetable products—food..	80.5	233.0	34
Fibers, textiles and textile products........	64.9	209.3	31
Non-ferrous metals and products..........	57.2	328.7	17
Animals, fish and other products..........	30.9	71.8	43
Agricultural and vegetable products— other than food......................	27.9	90.4	31
Totals.................................	1,541.7	3,998.4	39

1. Includes such items as machinery, engines and boilers, and vehicles and parts.
Source: Dominion Bureau of Statistics.

Duty-free Canadian Imports from the United States

As Table 2 indicates, almost two-fifths of all Canada's purchases from the United States during 1957 crossed the border without any payment of duty. A very large proportion of this free trade takes place in goods falling within the trade category "iron and its products", with the two most important items being farm equipment and certain automobile parts. For example, in 1956 (the most recent year for which statistics are available on an item basis), about $225 million worth of farm equipment entered Canada free of duty from the United States, accounting for virtually all the imports of this type of article from that country. In the same year, approximately $150 million worth of automobile parts entered duty-free, although another $125 million had to pay duty. In 1956, other important manufactures of iron or steel included well-drilling apparatus ($72 million), iron ore ($37 million), scrap for remelting ($34 million), well casing and tubing and certain aircraft engines and parts.

In the non-metallic minerals group, by far the most important item is coal. All anthracite coal enters duty-free, but bituminous only if it is to be converted into coke or is to be used in the production of synthetic rubber. Thus, in 1956, no duty was paid on the $24 million worth of anthracite coal purchased from the United States nor on $31 million of the $97 million of bituminous coal coming in. Other free items in this category include petroleum (no longer of great importance), sand and silica for the manufacture of glass, plate glass, phosphate rock and coke.

The value of trade in any single duty-free chemical or wood item is not large, the highest running around $5 to $10 million a year in such items as synthetic resins, aniline and coal-tar dyes, spraying chemicals and medicinal preparations. In the agricultural and vegetable products section in 1956, soya beans ($24 million), oranges ($23 million), and soya bean oil, cake and meal ($12 million) are the only large items.

Finally, a high percentage of goods in the miscellaneous category are duty-free, with three classes making up over half the value of trade in 1956: (1) aircraft, exclusive of engines ($83 million); (2) tourist purchases exempt from duty ($73 million); and (3) arms, military stores and munitions which are to remain the property of British Commonwealth or NATO countries ($45 million). Other items of interest in this group, although the value of trade in no case is very large, are scientific apparatus, surgical instruments, and X-ray equipment.

3

The System of Tariffs
and Quotas

U.S. Tariffs and Quotas

TARIFFS

The present U.S. tariff structure was established in 1930 by the Smoot-Hawley Act, although the classifications, basic rates and operating procedures established by this law have since been overlaid and modified by amending laws, administrative actions and legal decisions.

The Act is divided into four major titles. Title I, the Dutiable List, is divided into 15 Schedules of articles ranging from Chemicals, Oils and Paints (Schedule 1), to a "catch-all" classification called Sundries (Schedule 15). Title II, the shortest section of the four, is the Free List. Title III, "Special Administrative Provisions", modifies the structure and duties of the U.S. Tariff Commission and spells out provisions with regard to insular possessions, marking, countervailing duties, immoral articles, convict-made goods, sanitary regulations (to be administered by the Department of Agriculture), supplies for international vessels or planes, merchandise in bond, drawbacks and refunds, reimportation of tax-free exports, and property of sunken and abandoned vessels. Title IV, "Administrative Provisions", lays out the procedure for valuation, classification and recovering of duties. Regulations concerning transportation in bond and warehousing of merchandise are also included in this Title.

Tariff Classifications

The classification of tariff rates established by the Smoot-Hawley Act has been called tedious, archaic, ambiguous, hopelessly complex and virtually impossible to administer. It is truly all of these! The 15 schedules of Title I can be broken down into some 8,000 different rates.[1] Although this estimate is high when compared to other counts, it provides for only a small percentage of the total listings known to the trade. The U.S. Department of

---

1. Estimate made by the Randall Commission.

10

Commerce claims the number of dutiable items to be 3,300 "by the most acceptable basis for counting them". Because of the minute specifications this number can be multiplied infinitely. And the 264 basket clauses can be added to this.[1]

The commodity classes are most frequently established according to the "chief value"—principal material in terms of value of which individual items are made. A golfer's caddy-cart with a wooden frame may be admitted as a wood product, while one with an aluminum frame may be subject to duty as a manufacture of metal at a totally different rate. However, the tariff status may depend upon whether an article is "in part of" a specified material, such as asbestos, bamboo, etc. Designation by name also occurs—"wiping rags", "handkerchiefs", "mufflers", "pickets", "posts", etc.

Finally, it is not uncommon for articles to be described in terms of their use in the United States—dyeing and tanning extracts, perfume materials, flavouring extracts, healing plasters. It is important to distinguish whether such descriptions apply to the intention of the foreign designer or producer; to the use intended by the importer and the fulfillment of this intention by the article being so used after importation; to the chief use in the United States at the time of importation; to the chief use at the time of enactment of the tariff provision; or to the suitability of certain items for particular uses. No uniform rule will apply in every case.

There are, of course, other tariff terms and descriptive methods—for example, leather gloves are classed not only by types of leather, but also by methods of seaming, types of trim, and length. Over 125 classifications of leather gloves appear in the schedule.

Columns of Rates

Discrimination by the United States toward some countries is evident in both the structure and the administration of the tariff. In the case of specified articles, lower rates and other preferential favors are given to both Cuba and the Philippines; and, since 1951, imports from designated Communist countries or areas have not enjoyed Most-Favoured-Nation (MFN) treatment, but pay the rates provided for in the 1930 Smoot-Hawley Act. These three exceptions apart, the tariff is extended to all nations at the rates established under reciprocal trade agreements, including those established through negotiations under the General Agreement on Tariffs and Trade (GATT).

Cuban Preference. Selected Cuban products are given preferential rates below those established by the MFN procedures; other products not described in the U.S. tariff schedules are accorded preferential rates of duty by

---

1. A basket clause provides for all those goods which are not enumerated in more specific language.

virtue of the fact that they are of a class or kind which was imported in specified "key" years preceding the exclusive agreement.[1]

Philippine Trade Agreement. In accordance with the terms of a bilateral trade agreement, the concessions accorded to certain Philippine products are being reduced by a specified percentage over a 20-year period ending in 1974. At that time, the Philippines will be accorded only the MFN rates.

Insular Possessions. The customs area of the United States extends beyond the territorial limits of the 50 states to include only Puerto Rico. Special regulations apply to other insular possessions and the Canal Zone.

The Problem of Applicable Rates

An added complication is the variety of formulas provided by law in specifying duty rates. One effect is to obscure the true relation between the amount of the duty and the value of the goods that is, the ad valorem equivalent. A few examples drawn from the schedule will help to illustrate the nature of this problem.

Simple duties, specific or ad valorem, are the easiest to understand. When both of these duties are applied to a single commodity, the rate is called a compound duty (fountain pens have a specific duty of five cents each plus a 34 percent ad valorem duty).

Some classifications have been made by value brackets. A common reason for utilizing more complicated types of classification is to qualify concessions made in trade agreements. Examples include new classifications of bicycles to accomodate only British-type cycles with narrow tires and light frames; division of a basket clause on chemicals into six groups, each with a separate rate of duty; and breaking down the paragraph covering dolls and toys from five to 30 sub-groups.

Value-bracket classifications can be specific, ad valorem or compound. A compound case, in which both the specific and ad valorem rates vary with the value, is illustrated below:

Item	Duty
Shotguns valued at over $10, but not over $25 —	$2 plus 15 percent ad valorem
Shotguns valued at over $25, but not over $50 —	$2.55 plus 12½ percent ad valorem

Maximum and minimum rates may be established for ad valorem duties and these duties may also be of a compound nature:

Item		Duty
Braid suitable for hat-making containing a substantial part of synthetic textile, but not in chief value thereof	24¢ per pound	minimum ad valorem of 22½ percent, or not more than 45 percent ad valorem

1. Preferential duty rates for Cuban products need no longer be embodied in exclusive agreements with Cuba alone.

Generally, both maximum and minimum ad valorem rates tend to discriminate against the cheaper lines of products. To belabour the obvious, value brackets also discriminate—for example, shotguns costing $26 and $49 will both be placed in the value bracket of $25 to $50, and both are subject to the same specific tariff of $2.55.

Another aspect of the problem of applicable rates has to do with determining the major component of an item in terms of value—that is, the "chief value". An example of this would be a hat body composed of three percent or more angora and 97 percent wool. The ad valorem duty rate would be applied to the more expensive ingredient, angora. To further complicate the schedule, maximum and minimum amounts of the materials may be established—that is, if that hat contained less than three percent angora fur, it would not be valued on the basis of the price of angora, but on the basis of that for wool hat bodies. Price changes can, of course, cause changes in the item of "chief value", leading to a different rate of duty. This has occurred in the case of textiles of mixed fibers, such as rayon and cotton.

Rates on items "in part of" specified materials can be even more difficult than the "chief value" provisions. For instance, synthetic rubber tires containing a small percentage of carbon have, in the past, been classified as articles "in part of" carbon. A plain cotton table spread is dutiable at a rate of 12½ percent, but cotton spreads with fringe are dutiable at the rate for cotton fringe, or 42 percent. Under this rule of classification, wearing apparel or even toy dolls can become "in part of" braid, lace, or embroidery if an insignificant piece of such materials is attached to them, and can be assessed at a much higher rate of duty.

Products not enumerated in the tariff schedules (generally new products, such as plastic articles) may be classified under the "rule of similitude", which provides that any new article not enumerated in the Tariff Act but similar to another product enumerated in the Act, with respect to the use to which it may be applied, will be accorded a similar rate of duty. If, however, it should resemble two or more products, the rate of duty accorded would be that which it most resembles with respect to the materials of which it is composed.

These complex and rigid rules give rise to numerous anomalies. An extreme example relates to certain one millimeter metal balls used as points of ball point pens. These were classified as parts of fountain pens dutiable at the rate of 72 cents per dozen plus 40 percent ad valorem—about 2400 percent of their commercial value.

Import-Excise and Processing Taxes

One might surmise at this point that we have covered the full gamut of taxes on imports. This is not so. There are a number of other taxes in existence which play an additional and significant role in the U.S. tariff structure.

Import-excise and processing taxes serve a number of purposes, such as to compensate for domestic excise taxes and to provide temporary protection without amending the Tariff Act. These taxes, which originated in 1932, have been imposed on such products as lumber, copper ores and articles containing copper, oil seeds, petroleum and derivatives and coal.

The Tariff Commission, however, does not incorporate these taxes into its tariff schedules, although it does call attention to the import tax in a footnote with a general warning that "the absence of a footnote for a particular product does not necessarily mean that the product is exempt from import tax". In addition, the classification descriptions of products subject to import tax are usually unlike the tariff-act classification descriptions, and import taxes may be imposed on different units—for example, weight in one case and linear measure in another.

Some imports are discriminated against under the rules for applying these additional taxes. For example, the import tax on distilled spirits is $10.50 on each proof gallon, or wine gallon when below proof. Bottled Canadian whiskey is below proof, hence the excise tax is higher than that paid by American producers of similar whiskeys. Domestic spirits are taxed on the basis of proof gallons. The added tax paid by Canadian whiskeys depends on the price of bottled goods and their alcoholic content. It is estimated to average about 20 cents per fifth.

Special fees on agricultural products for which domestic price support programs are in effect are another feature of the structure of tariffs. These may be imposed whenever the Secretary of Agriculture believes that imports might interfere with a domestic program. Although the Secretary has tended to rely on quotas rather than on such fees, they are currently in effect on almonds (in excess of five million pounds per year), on peanut oil (in excess of 80 million pounds), and on flaxseed and linseed oil.

Nuisance Duties

One feature of the U.S. tariff structure is the persistence of very low duties on a number of major imports. This is primarily the result of a feature of the 1930 Tariff Act which prohibits transfer of any commodity to the free list. Owing to price increases since 1930 and duty reductions under the Reciprocal Trade Agreements Program, the ad valorem equivalent of many specific duties has dropped almost to the vanishing point.

More than 100 commodities are imported from Canada with duties under two percent ad valorem equivalent. Imports from Canada subjected to nuisance duties in 1957 totalled $350 million—the principal items were nickel, lumber, fish and numerous primary iron and steel products. Other commodities of this type are scattered throughout the tariff schedule. Examples are: strawberries, flower seed, peat moss, babbit metal and solder, soda ash, caustic soda, and horse shoes. In most cases, these duties are so low that neither their protectionist effect nor their customs revenues are of any significance.

Table 3 summarizes the available data on U.S. duties on imports from Canada. As is the case with respect to all averages, these statistics tend to smooth out the humps and valleys. Any such figures should, of course, be used with great caution. Their significance, for example, is limited by the fact that average rates of duty on actual imports are biased downwards by the existence of high individual duties which greatly curtail or exclude certain imports. In the extreme cases where prohibitive duties exclude all imports, the ratio of duties collected to imports would be equal to zero.

Moreover, any interpretation of these statistics must take into account the fact that certain items, such as lead and zinc, and many agricultural products and foodstuffs are affected not only by tariffs but also by restrictive quotas, sanitary and marking regulations and other trade obstacles. Low tariffs in these cases may be relatively unimportant.

On the other hand, the height of the tariffs at any given time may overstate its protective effects against Canadian competition in those cases where

TABLE 3

U.S. Dutiable Imports from Canada, and Duties Collected, by Commodity Groups, Year Ending June 30, 1957

Commodity Group	Dutiable Imports	Total Imports	Duties Collected	Duties Collected As a Percent of: Dutiable Imports	All Imports
	(Millions of Dollars)				
Metals and manufactures, except machinery and vehicles....................	337.2	714.2	15.7	5	2
Wood and paper..............	280.4	1,254.3	7.0	2	1
Non-metallic minerals	170.2	278.5	7.0	4	3
Vegetable food products and beverages.................	161.0	174.5	19.1	12	11
Animals and animal products, edible......................	97.7	119.1	5.4	6	5
Machinery and vehicles........	41.6	136.9	5.5	13	4
Chemicals and related products.	29.7	85.0	4.4	15	5
Vegetable products, inedible, except fibers and wood.......	13.3	16.2	1.0	8	6
Miscellaneous................	11.7	107.5	1.3	11	1
Animals and animal products, inedible....................	11.1	45.8	1.0	9	2
Textile fibers and manufactures.	3.9	10.1	0.7	18	7
Adjustments[1]................	29.9	35.0	N.A.	—	—
Totals....................	1,187.7	2,977.1	68.1[2]	6[3]	2[3]

1. Shipments individually valued at $250 or less not classified.
2. Excludes duties collected on shipments individually valued at $250 or less.
3. On the basis of unadjusted totals.
Source: U.S. Bureau of Customs. For explanation of coverage and sampling procedure, see U.S. Department of Commerce, Bureau of the Census: *Report No. FT 120, United States Imports of Merchandise for Consumption*, Government Printing Office, Washington, D.C., (Monthly).

15

Canadian costs are higher than costs in the United States. These and other considerations make it evident that the statistics are so inadequate as a basis for analysis that intensive studies of a number of industries are required before clear assessments can be made as to whether current trade barriers are an obstacle to increased imports. About all that can be concluded from Table 3 is that the dutiable items that do enter in quantity are generally, though not always, those bearing low rates. However, at least a few types of imports enter the United States over very high tariff barriers—for example, in the case of some vegetable food products and beverages (particularly baked articles, jellies and jams and alcoholic beverages), and automotive and aircraft specialties (included in the "machinery and vehicles" category). The effects of tariffs and trade barriers on these and other industries are examined in greater detail in Chapter 6.

QUOTAS

A quota is similar in many respects to a tariff duty, and it almost invariably tends to maintain or raise the domestic price above that prevailing abroad.[1] Two types of quotas are in common use by the United States: (1) tariff-rate quotas and (2) absolute quotas.

The tariff quota allows a specified quantity of a commodity to enter under a special rate of duty during a given period, and any additional amount is free to enter at a higher rate. An example is the tariff on potatoes of 37½ cents per hundredweight, to a maximum of 1,900,000 bushels in any one year for seed potatoes and 600,000 bushels for table stock. Imports over these amounts are assessed 75 cents duty per hundredweight.

Tariff-rate quotas currently exist for the following products: fresh or sour cream, fresh or sour whole milk, live cattle, fresh or frozen fish fillets, tuna fish, seed and table stock potatoes, walnuts, peanut oil and worsted and woolen fabrics.

The Mechanics of Quotas

The tariff-rate quotas are all global—that is to say, specific amounts are not assigned to each country exporting a given commodity to the United States. Absolute quotas are also global, with the exception of those applying to tung oil and tung nuts, short-staple cotton, cotton waste, wheat and wheat flour, rye, rye meal and rye flour, lead and zinc ores, and smelter products.

Absolute quotas place a limit on the importation of a product during a quota period (generally one year). Quotas allocated to individual countries may be based on their percentage contribution to total U.S. imports during some base period. However, many of the quotas assigned to individual countries may be merely nominal, in order to avoid giving the impression that the country's exports are being embargoed.

---

1. Although this may not be true in the case of an industry in which a consequent expansion of domestic production may permit greater efficiencies.

An example of an allocated quota is shown in Table 4, which shows the quantities of wheat and wheat flour authorized to be entered or withdrawn from warehouses during any one year for consumption under the import quotas for these two commodities. The quota period for wheat and flour begins on May 29 of each year.

TABLE 4

U.S. Quotas for Wheat and Wheat Flour

Country of Origin	Wheat (bu.)	Wheat Flour (lbs.)
Canada...	795,000	3,815,000
29 other countries[1]................................	5,000	185,000
Sum of country quotas..........................	800,000	4,000,000

1. Thirteen countries have wheat quotas and 24 countries have wheat flour quotas.

In the case of each commodity, the quota period depends upon the date of the Presidential proclamation imposing the quota. Seasonal quotas are in effect for certain commodities in order to provide for milder restrictions during periods of lower production. For example, the tariff rate on butter is seven cents per pound on imports from November 1 to March 31, on a quantity not to exceed 50 million pounds during the quota period. The quota is reduced to five million pounds during two periods ending July 15 and October 31; imports in excess of these quotas must pay the full rate of 14 cents per pound. Although special exceptions are made during bad crop years, the effective quota period of all seasonal absolute and tariff quotas are fixed by law.

Prevalence and Restrictiveness of Quotas

Quotas are most extensive with respect to agricultural products, particularly those for which a domestic price-support program exists. With the exception of absolute quotas on oil, lead and zinc, and on certain imports from the Philippines, all quotas now in effect are on agricultural commodities. Since the tariff quotas have been discussed above, we are concerned here only with absolute quotas.

Dairy products. Quotas are in effect on dried cream, butter, dried whole milk, dried buttermilk, malted milk and compounds, dried skim milk, Cheddar cheese, blue-mold cheese, Edam and Gouda cheese, Italian (cow's milk) cheese, butter oil and butter substitutes. For all other dairy products containing 45 percent or more butterfat—except cheeses, evaporated and condensed milk, and products imported in retail packages—no imports are authorized, since it was determined in effect that there was no representative base period.

Section 22 of the Agricultural Adjustment Act, which authorized the imposition of these quotas, does not allow embargoes to be imposed on

17

agricultural commodities. The pertinent language is as follows: "no proclamation under this section shall impose any limitation on the total quantity of any article or articles which may be entered . . . which reduces such permissible total quantity to proportionately less than 50 per centum of the total quantity of such article or articles which was entered . . . during a representative period as determined by the President".

Quotas must be maintained in effect on dairy products so long as legislation requires price support at high levels to producers. Since April 1, 1959, the support prices have been $3.06 per hundredweight for manufacturing milk, and 56.6 cents per pound for butterfat in farm-separated cream. As shown in Table 5, U.S. market prices of dairy products at levels corresponding to these levels of support, are well above the prices of dairy products in the major dairy-exporting countries.

TABLE 5

U.S. Absolute Quotas and U.S. Prices, as Percentages of World Prices, Selected Agricultural Commodities

Commodity	Quota	U.S. Price as a Percent of World Price[1]
Wheat fit for human consumption (bu.).......	800,000[2]	132
Wheat milling products (bu.)...............	4,000,000[2]	131
Butter (lbs.).............................	707,000[3]	174
Dried whole milk (lbs.)....................	7,000[3]	122 to 163
Dried skim milk (lbs.).....................	1,807,000[3]	142 to 213
Blue-mold cheese (lbs.)....................	4,167,000[3]	123 to 138
Cheddar cheese and cheese substitutes containing Cheddar (lbs.)................	2,780,100[3]	86 to 147
Edam and Gouda cheese (lbs.)..............	4,600,200[3]	149 to 188
Tung oil and tung nuts (lbs.)...............	26,000,000[2]	208
Rye, rye flour and rye meal (lbs.)...........	186,000,000[4]	133

1. As of December 1958.
2. Sum of country quotas.
3. Global quota.
4. For 12-month period commencing July 1, 1960. Current quota for 10-month period beginning September 1, 1959, is 77,399,736 pounds, of which not more than 5,939 pounds shall be rye flour or meal.

Since the law provides that support be carried out by loans on purchases of milk and its products, government price support purchases would obviously rise if imports were to increase substantially.

Industrial raw materials and fuels. The U.S. quotas on lead and zinc ores, concentrates and refined metal are discussed in Chapter 5. Their effects on U.S. price levels are indicated in Table 6. It should be noted that these effects derive both from increasing reliance on higher-cost domestic sources of supply and from the diversion of supplies to other markets. Moreover, since all of these items are subject to import taxes or tariffs, the higher U.S. prices are attributable in part to them. The U.S. also has global quotas on petroleum, but in 1959 Canada was, with minor limitations, exempted from them.

TABLE 6

U.S. Absolute Quotas and U.S. Prices, as Percentages of World Prices, Selected Industrial Raw Materials and Fuels

Commodity	Quota	U.S. Price as a Percent of World Price[1]
Crude and unfinished oils (bbls./day)[2,3].........	936,770	121[4]
Residual fuel oil (bbls./day)[2]..................	347,311	102[5]
Finished petroleum products (bbls./day)[2,6].......	76,646	N.A.
Lead-bearing ores, flue dust, mattes (tons lead content)......................	33,040[7]	N.A.
Lead smelter products (tons)[8].................	55,600[7]	146
Zinc-bearing ores, except pyrites containing less than 3% zinc (tons zinc content)........	94,960[7]	N.A.
Zinc blocks, pigs or slabs, and zinc dust (tons)...	35,280[7]	106

1. As of December 1959.
2. Oil Import Administration allocations for the period April 1-June 30, 1959, exclusive of Puerto Rico. Overland imports from Canada are currently exempted, with minor limitations.
3. Includes products which are to be further processed other than by blending by mechanical means.
4. Laid-down cost at Philadelphia. W. Texas sour crude 35° A.P.I./ Arabian 35° A.P.I., duty included.
5. Laid-down price, U.S. Atlantic seaboard points for residual fuel oil from Texas Gulf Coast/ Carribean fuel oil of the same grade, duty included.
6. Includes products to be used without further processing except blending by mechanical means.
7. Sum of country quotas.
8. Lead bullion or base bullion, lead in pigs and bars, lead dross, reclaimed lead, scrap lead, antimonial lead, antimonial scrap lead, type metal, babbit metal solder, all alloys or combinations of lead not specifically provided for.

Canadian Tariffs and Import Controls

TARIFFS

Schedule A of the Customs Tariff states the rates of duty for each tariff item and Schedule B lists the goods eligible for various drawbacks of duty. Under Schedule A, there are three columns: the British Preferential Rate, the Most-Favoured-Nation Rate and the General Tariff Rate. An article must be substantially produced by the country entitled to the rate concerned and must be shipped directly to Canada. "Substantially produced" generally means 50 percent of the cost of production (although 25 percent or even less is occasionally deemed acceptable), as established by Cabinet Order in Council. In actual fact, the third column is no longer of any significance, since none of the countries trading with Canada to any real extent are subject to it. Therefore, for all practical purposes, Canada has a two-column tariff structure.

The Significance of British Preference

The United States and other countries not in the British Commonwealth come under the Most-Favoured-Nation Tariff. British Preference (BP) rates are sometimes equal but usually lower than corresponding Most-Favoured-Nation (MFN) rates. In 1951, of the 2,038 items and sub-items in the Canadian tariff, 1,450 had a lower BP than MFN rate. Where the BP rate is lower, the spread varies from a very narrow, as in the case of manufactures of wood not otherwise provided for (BP 17½ percent, MFN 20 percent) to a much wider spread, such as BP Free, MFN 17½ percent for automobiles, trucks and buses.

For a few commodities, the British preferential rates may have discriminatory effects on U.S. exporters, but it is reasonable to conclude that, in general, the preferential system does not swing Canadian purchases away from U.S. sources to any large extent. In 1958, for example, only 14 percent of total Canadian imports were from Commonwealth countries, as compared with 69 percent from the United States. Moreover, there are a great many imports from Commonwealth countries which do not depend on preferential tariff treatment to compete effectively with American producers. Such imports would include raw wool from Australia, New Zealand and the United Kingdom; wool manufactures from the United Kingdom; tropical agricultural products, such as crude rubber from Malaya and bananas from British Honduras; Scotch whiskey and many other alcoholic beverages; and a long list of manufactured items from the United Kingdom. Therefore, although the cessation of British preferential treatment would unquestionably seriously affect certain Commonwealth exports to Canada, such as automobiles, electrical apparatus, non-agricultural machinery, engines and boilers, and clay products, it would only be of marginal importance to U.S. producers.

The Tariff Structure

The tariff structure is complex and highly specialized, as the number of items mentioned above indicates. Demands for particular protection by the various segments of many industries have led to greater tariff specialization, as has the desire to narrow as much as possible the concessions made in international trade negotiations. The Torquay negotiations in 1951, for example, led to the addition of about 100 new items. The manner of classifying items in the tariff schedules is extremely complicated, with a given item frequently bearing more than one rate depending on such matters as its end use, whether it is of a type which is made in Canada or not, and, in the case of fresh fruits and vegetables grown in Canada, even on the particular season of the year.

A further complicating feature of the tariff structure is the variety of ways in which the rate of duty is stated. Most rates are ad valorem, meaning a payment equal to a certain proportion of the value of the goods; some are specific rates, that is, a fixed payment for a given quantity of goods; and others are a combination of these two.

Over-all Tariff Levels

There is a wide dispersion in the height of Canadian tariff rates. Along with the many free rates are very low ones, such as MFN five percent on blocks, pigs, or bars of tin. At the other end of the scale are a few exceptionally high rates, usually specific duties on goods of relatively low value. To illustrate the high rates, tariff item 232 provides for MFN rates of 22½ percent and five cents per pound on glue. For cheap glue valued at seven cents per pound, the ad valorem equivalent is quite steep; thus in 1954, the average ad valorem equivalent rate on powdered and sheet glue from the United States was 54 percent.

However, ad valorem equivalent rates over 50 percent are difficult to find. Only when the 40-percent level is reached do any really important commodities begin to appear. For example, rugs n.o.p. bear an MFN rate of 25 percent and five cents per square foot, which brought the average ad valorem equivalent on imports from the United States in 1954 to 40.5 percent. One needs to move even lower down the scale to the 30-35 percent level before the number of commercially important items begin to increase substantially. MFN rates range from 5 to 35 percent as a maximum (except where there are additional domestic excise duties). A great many important items bear an MFN rate of 22½ percent, including prepared roofings, paper of all kinds n.o.p., toilet soap, cosmetics, aluminum manufactures, washing machines, machinery n.o.p., railway cars, cooking and heating apparatus, electric light fixtures and appliances n.o.p., electric dynamos and motors, manufactures of iron and steel n.o.p., rubber boots and shoes and rubber tires and tubes. Another important group of items bear an MFN rate of 17½ percent—automobiles, trucks and buses; bleached and printed cotton fabrics; cotton yarn; and frozen vegetables. But there are also many items with much lower rates—such as plastics, window glass, structural steel, and office machinery. Many manufactures not produced in Canada bear MFN rates of 7½ percent.

One statistical measure of the over-all height of the Canadian tariff is the ratio of duty collected to the value of either total imports or dutiable imports. As already indicated above, however, such ratios must be used with caution and may give a misleading impression of the restrictiveness of the tariffs. During 1957, for example, the ratio of duty collected to total imports from the United States was 10.2 percent. In the same year, the ratio of duty collected to the value of dutiable imports alone was 16.6 percent. Table 7 shows the average ad valorem rates on imports from the United States during 1957 by commodity groups.

IMPORT CONTROLS

Although there is no actual import quota system in Canada, there are certain statutory provisions for the prohibition or limitation of selected items.

Prohibited Items

Schedule C of the Customs Tariff lists certain items which are prohibited from entry. Most of these are types of articles which one would expect to find on such a list, including books, drawings and photographs of a "treasonable or seditious, or of an immoral or indecent character", base or counterfeit coin, animals suffering from contagious diseases, reprints of Canadian copyrighted books, goods produced by prison labour, and posters depicting scenes of crime and violence.

TABLE 7

Dutiable Imports into Canada from the United States, and Duties Collected by Commodity Groups, 1957

Commodity Group	Total Imports	Dutiable Imports	Duties Collected	Duties Collected As a Percent of: Dutiable Imports	Total Imports
	(Millions of Dollars)				
Iron and its products[1]..........	1,802.0	1,164.9	182.6	16	10
Miscellaneous................	417.7	155.2	32.1	21	8
Non-metallic minerals.........	391.3	220.2	22.9	10	6
Non-ferrous metals...........	328.7	271.5	54.9	20	17
Chemicals and allied products..	253.0	143.1	22.9	16	9
Agricultural and vegetable products					
—mainly food..............	233.0	152.5	17.8	12	8
—other than food..........	90.4	62.5	13.3	21	15
Fibers, textiles and textile products.................	209.3	144.4	35.4	24	17
Wood, wood products and paper...................	201.2	101.5	19.7	19	10
Animals, fish and their products................	71.8	40.9	5.8	14	8
Total......................	3,998.4	2,456.7	407.1	17	10

1. Includes such items as machinery, engines and boilers, and vehicles and parts.
Source: Compiled from data supplied by the Dominion Bureau of Statistics.

Three items on the list, however, call for special attention—oleomargarine, used or second-hand automobiles, and used or second-hand aircraft. In the case of oleomargarine, there is no doubt that substantial imports would move in from the United States if the prohibition were lifted, since the U.S. price is significantly lower than the Canadian price. The prohibition, which, incidentally, has been in effect since 1886, is intended to protect domestic producers of butter rather than margarine. The ingredients of butter substitutes may be imported into those provinces which permit the manufacture of margarine.

The prohibition on used or second-hand automobiles or other used vehicles manufactured prior to the year in which importation is sought (except in special circumstances) similarly cuts off considerable trade with the United States. Restricted entry of used cars was deemed necessary in order to make effective the tariff on new automobiles. Since a tariff on used automobiles would be extremely difficult to administer due to valuation difficulties, an outright ban was imposed.

Import Controls on Agricultural Commodities

The Export and Import Permits Act enables the Cabinet to establish an import control list which may include any article, the import of which the Cabinet deems necessary to control for certain purposes. The most important purpose is to implement action taken under Federal farm stabilization legislation to support the domestic price of a commodity—for example, The Agricultural Stabilization Act. At the present time, import curbs are in effect for butter, butter fat, cheddar cheese, dried skim milk and turkeys, and there are little or no commercial imports. There was an import quota of 300,000 pounds for broiler turkeys during the period October 27 to December 31, 1958, very much below normal holiday season marketings; and of one million pounds during the period July 1 to September 30, 1959.

Another reason for such controls is to implement an intergovernmental arrangement or commitment. Tin was on the control list for this purpose until March 1959, when it was removed because Russia reached an agreement with the International Tin Council to limit tin exports. Thus, the agricultural products noted above are now the only commodities whose importation is controlled under the Export and Import Permits Act.

To what extent does this control restrict importation from the United States? In the case of butter and dried skim milk, the answer is likely not very much, since New Zealand is more competitive on world markets than the United States. On the other hand, a relaxation of controls on turkeys would probably stimulate much larger purchases from U.S. suppliers. In 1956, before turkeys were placed on the control list, all Canada's foreign turkey-buying was done in the United States, the value of imports amounting to $5,362,000.

Similarly, there would likely be a significant increase in the cheddar cheese imports from the United States as well as from other countries, such as Switzerland, Italy and Denmark. In 1956, before cheddar cheese was placed under import control, Canada's imports were valued at $4,163,000: $1,050,000 came from Switzerland; $879,000, from Italy; $729,000, from Denmark; and $633,000, from the United States.

A third statute enabling the control of imports is the Canadian Wheat Board Act, which gives the Board authority to license imports of wheat, oats, and barley, and any product containing more than 25 percent of these grains by weight. At the present time, imports of the following commodities are subject to license by the Board: wheat, wheat flour, and wheat starch; oats, including ground, crimped, crushed, rolled, and meal; and barley, including ground, crimped, meal, and flour. For a time in 1957 and 1958, it was necessary to obtain a license for a variety of other products, including cakes, cake mixes, macaroni, and animal feeds. The Board took the view that because of the large supplies of grain in Canada at that time, they would not issue permits for grain products which could be obtained from Canadian sources. When application was made for the importation of any new product of this kind, detailed information was required, including an assurance that it met a specific market in Canada and was not available domestically.

Miscellaneous Import Controls

There are a number of other types of import control used in Canada. Under the Atomic Energy Control Act, import permits are required for the importation of fissionable materials and radio-active isotopes or any equipment which may be used for the production, use, or application of atomic energy. This control is for strategic rather than commercial purposes.

In provinces which have established government liquor stores—all but Manitoba and Prince Edward Island—provincial import licenses must be obtained. However, most provincial liquor-control boards are willing to give hotels and clubs permits to import private stock.

4

Administrative Protectionism in the United States

ONE EFFECT of almost any government regulation of business, whatever its original purpose, is that it is likely to make it more difficult to import goods and services from abroad. At times, such regulations contain outright discrimination against foreign goods. Incidental protectionist effects result, for example, from legislation concerning copyright and trade-mark provisions, food, drug, and health regulations, "fair trade" or "anti-dumping" laws, and many others. Other regulations, directed specifically at controlling the importation of goods, may cause unnecessary expense and inconvenience in clearing customs, establish valuations for customs purposes higher than the prices for which goods are sold for export, or may open the door to improper use of dumping and other punitive duties. Barriers to trade which arise in this fashion form what is virtually an "invisible tariff", and may well constitute much more effective trade obstacles than customs duties.

Valuation, classification and anti-dumping provisions have aspects which are clearly in the public interest. A value must usually be established, as the amount of ad valorem and specific value-bracket duties are dependent on it. Also, without proper valuation of goods, dumping and other penalty duties cannot be fairly established, and meaningful trade statistics cannot be assembled. Because so much is dependent on valuation, a great deal of serious effort has gone into establishing valuation procedures.

Activities of administrative officials in classifying merchandise are also of vital importance to importers. As illustrated in Chapter 3, the complexities of tariff legislation make it possible for classification to be the determining factor as to whether an item of imported merchandise can be profitably sold. Disputes constantly arise from the fact that foreign exporters, domestic importers, and customs officials differ as to which tariff paragraph applies to the merchandise at hand. In fact, different customs offices frequently make different decisions about the same type of merchandise.

Government Agencies Involved

Before turning to an examination of administrative barriers, let us briefly look at the institutional framework within which they operate. Agencies in charge of the day-to-day operations of U.S. foreign trade activities are numerous, with multiple lines of authority. Executive authority is often shared among agencies.

The U.S. Treasury influences U.S. imports through the following key agencies:

BUREAU OF CUSTOMS. The Bureau's principal function is the assessment and collection of import duties, and, incident to this, the prevention of smuggling. The Bureau cooperates with other Government agencies in enforcing the preventive, sanitary, and other laws relating to articles brought into the United States. It also acts as an agent of the Internal Revenue Service in collecting excise taxes.

DIVISION OF FOREIGN ASSETS CONTROL. The Division administers the Foreign Assets Control Regulations under the Trading With the Enemy Act. The major purpose of the regulations is to prevent the Chinese Communist authorities from utilizing their dollar assets in the United States, and to preclude the acquisition by those authorities of U.S. dollars. This Division also administers regulations which prohibit persons in the United States from engaging in certain transactions involving the shipment of merchandise from foreign countries to Russia or other Communist countries.

Other Departments influence U.S. imports through the following agencies:
DEPARTMENT OF HEALTH, EDUCATION AND WELFARE, FOOD AND DRUG ADMINISTRATION. This agency maintains surveillance over traffic subject to the Food, Drug and Cosmetic Act.

DEPARTMENT OF AGRICULTURE (Various Divisions). Fees and quotas imposed under the Agricultural Adjustment Act have been discussed above. Authority for declaring that imports are interfering with a program of the Department of Agriculture, or are practically certain to do so, rests with the Secretary of Agriculture. In such cases, the Tariff Commission may be directed to conduct a public hearing and make a recommendation to the President for action with regard to import fees or quotas.

The Department of Agriculture also administers specific legislation, such as the Animal and Plant Quarantine Acts, the Insect Pest Act, the Honeybee Importation Act, the Virus-Serum Toxin Act, the Import Meat Act, portions of the Tariff Act of 1930 with regard to the introduction into the United States of rinderpest and hoof-and-mouth disease and regulations covering the importation of animal by-products.

OFFICE OF CIVIL AND DEFENSE MOBILIZATION. This agency influences imports through a number of powers. Under the Strategic and

Critical Materials Stockpiling Act, it must determine from time to time which materials are strategic and critical and the quality and quantities of such materials which shall be stockpiled. Under the Trade Agreements Extension Act of 1955, whenever the Director of OCDM has reason to believe that any article is being imported into the United States in such quantities as to threaten to impair the national security, he shall so advise the President. If the President agrees that there is reason for such belief, he shall authorize an investigation to determine the facts. The President is authorized in such cases to take such steps as may be indicated to adjust imports.

TARIFF COMMISSION. The Commission performs few executive duties, although its influence with regard to over-all trade policy is substantial. Its primary function is to investigate and report upon tariff and foreign trade matters, as required by a number of statutes, including the Tariff Act, the Agricultural Adjustment Act, and the Antidumping Act. The Commission reports to the President and to Congress.

UNITED STATES CUSTOMS COURT. This is an administrative court which hears appeals from decisions of customs officials. Appeals from the Court's decisions, on matters of law only, are made to the United States Court of Customs and Patent Appeals. Administrative decisions with regard to both valuation and classification are appealed to this court, not only by the parties directly affected but also by domestic producers, who are thereby granted a powerful weapon for harassing foreign competitors.

Valuation Legislation and Procedures

The manner in which the statutory bases of customs valuation shall be applied is expressly prescribed in the Customs Simplification Act of 1956, and there is no administrative discretion whatever in this matter. These bases are:

"(1) the export value, or

"(2) if the export value cannot be determined satisfactorily, then the United States value, or

"(3) if neither the export value nor the United States value can be determined satisfactorily, then the constructed value; except that, in the case of an imported article subject to a rate of duty based on the American selling price of a domestic article, such value shall be

"(4) the American selling price of such domestic article".

Each of these four bases of valuation are carefully defined in the law, in an attempt to minimize litigation over such troublesome phrases as "freely sold", "ordinary course of trade", "purchasers at wholesale", "such or similar merchandise", "usual wholesale quantities", "transactions between related persons" and the like.

So far as the export value is concerned, the most important applications are as follows:

• Value is equivalent to the price at which identical or similar merchandise was sold, or, in the absence of sales, offered for sale at wholesale, in the ordinary course of trade, to one or more selected purchasers for export to the United States. "Selected purchasers" may be exclusive selling agents or representatives, provided the price involved in the transaction fairly represents the market value of the merchandise without undue restrictions as to its disposition or use.

• The price is normally that at which sales are made to purchasers in the usual wholesale quantities, either for industrial use or for re-sale. Sales to retailers are only considered when there are no sales or offers to wholesalers or to industrial users.

• In cases where sales are made at different prices for different wholesale quantities, the term "usual wholesale quantities" means that quantity representing the greatest aggregate volume of sales during a representative period.

• If the item is offered to selected purchasers, the Bureau of Customs must sometimes make a field investigation to determine whether the price offered to selected purchasers reflects the true value of the merchandise—that is, whether the export price varies from the domestic price for legitimate reasons, such as greater volume or less advertising and promotion activities on sales in the United States than abroad. In other cases, the customs appraiser can usually determine export value from the price stated on the customs invoice.

Since the legislation outlined above is new, we have very little to go on by way of determining what uncertainties and delays may be involved in determining the value for duty purposes. The importer is required to advance the estimated amount of duty, pending liquidation of the invoice. It is evident from the following statistics that this procedure is responsible for considerable delay and uncertainty for some importers.

TABLE 8

Invoices on Hand Over 90 Days in Offices of Appraisers,
1952 and 1958

Reason for Delay	June 30, 1952	Sept. 30, 1958
Foreign inquiry report.....................	34,831	17,115
Action by examiner........................	22,016	67,291
Court action on related cases...............	10,805	1,685
Reply from Customs Information Exchange...	10,466	38,138
Amendment by importer...................	6,276	[2]
Information from importer.................	5,752	17,109
Customs invoice..........................	1,960[1]	972
All other causes..........................	7,642	42,989
Total...................................	99,748	185,299

1. Consular invoice.
2. Included in "all other causes".
Source: U.S. Treasury Department, Bureau of Customs.

TABLE 9

Reappraisement Appeals, U.S. Customs Court, Fiscal Years 1952 to 1959

Year	Pending Beginning of Year	Received During Year	Decided During Year	Pending Close of Year
1952..............	48,931	14,977	961	62,947
1954..............	64,657	6,022	2,496	68,282
1956..............	79,940	18,572	13,627	84,885
1958..............	75,854	26,842	16,028	86,668
1959..............	86,668	22,376	20,663	88,381

Source: Administrative Office of the U.S. Courts, *Annual Report of the Director*, Washington, D.C.

Although the backlog in both administrative and judicial procedures has rapidly grown to unbelievable levels, some measure of improvement is expected as a result of the simplifications introduced under the Customs Simplification Act of 1956. However, customs administration is still badly handicapped by an arbitrary provision of the law.

Congress was so impressed with the protective effects of the old valuation procedures that in enacting the change it provided for certain commodities to be exempted from the new definitions. Specifically, the simplified valuation bases are not to apply when the result is a reduction in dutiable value of five percent or more. The Treasury Department has issued a "final list" specifying the items which will be treated under the old basis, following a study indicating that the decrease in dutiable value which would have occurred ranged from insignificant amounts for some commodity groups to "as high as 30 to 40 percent, or in isolated cases, perhaps even more".[1]

The "final list" means just that. There is no provision for reviewing or eliminating a list of items comprising 15 percent of all commodity imports. For the time being, then, the United States is operating on a dual valuation system, with old, more ambiguous and more protective standards applicable to one group of commodities, and a modernized set of standards applicable to all other dutiable imports.

Other recent procedural reforms include:

• A simplified customs invoice for shipments in excess of $500, which does not have to be certified by an American Consul as heretofore.

• A decision by the Bureau of Customs to publish abstracts of rulings on different aspects of import procedures. This could lead to more frequent protests by domestic producers, and to litigation to prevent the Bureau's decisions from remaining in effect. It does, at the same time, give importers and foreign producers timely access to the facts.

---

1. National Council of American Importers, *Special Report on Customs Valuation*, New York, 1955, page 16.

• Introduction of the Canadian Query Program.[1]

In summary, despite notable progress in certain areas, the work of the Bureau is needlessly complicated by valuation law. As a result, much time is consumed in liquidating entries about which complex economic facts must be ascertained, and persons engaged in the import business are subjected to considerable financial risk.

Classification Procedures

The second important step in liquidation of an entry is determination of the amount of duty payable on imported goods, or their free status. This is known as classification—arriving at a conclusion as to the particular provision of the Tariff Act in which an item of merchandise is described.

---

1. "The primary reason for this program was to make readily available the services of an experienced customs officer to provide Canadian shippers, or prospective shippers, with reliable information as to value, classification, marking, and other phases of customs applicable to imports. Appraisers of merchandise and other customs officials, not only in the United States but also in U.S. Treasury offices abroad, have for years been furnishing advice to foreign exporters relative to shipping their merchandise into the United States. The only new feature of the Canadian Query Program is the visit to the shipper's plant upon request of the exporter or prospective exporter and the processing of the report resulting from the visit.

Because of his experience and proximity to the main industrial centers of Canada, Mr. E. J. Cannon, appraiser at Buffalo, was selected to implement this program which began to operate early in 1956.

The program was given a great deal of initial publicity in the Canadian press, trade journals, and similar media, and the response has been extremely gratifying. In little more than three years, Mr. Cannon has submitted 218 formal reports and has conferred with over 3,300 Canadian businessmen, manufacturers, exporters, or prospective exporters in group meetings and individually.

A procedure has been adopted which has proved exceedingly satisfactory in the furtherance of this program. At a conference with the individual exporter or prospective exporter, the product or products and their use and composition are discussed. The terms of sale, the method of distribution, the probable ports of entry, the price or prices, and any other circumstances surrounding the proposed transaction are also discussed, and the inquirer is made fully conversant with the marking regulations, Agriculture Department regulations, and other formalities that would be encountered on shipping to the United States. A complete report of all pertinent facts is submitted by Mr. Cannon to the Bureau of Customs, and a copy is forwarded to the appraisers at all prospective ports of entry. The report is analyzed by the interested ports, and after all are in concurrence as to the value at which the merchandise would be appraised (disagreements being resolved by the Bureau), the exporter or prospective exporter is informed. A slightly different procedure is followed in connection with the classification of the commodity. Thus, the Canadian firm is fully informed on these vital points prior to shipment.

The advice furnished the prospective shipper remains in effect as long as the circumstances outlined in the report prevail. The exporter or prospective exporter is requested to advise Mr. Cannon of any subsequent change in his product or in his method of sale, distribution, or price, and upon receipt of such information, a supplemental report is prepared, submitted, and circulated in the same manner." (From a letter by Mr. Ralph Kelly, Commissioner of Customs)

Administrative procedures for classification are not complex. The Bureau, when requested by traders and when supplied with adequate information, makes rulings concerning classification of articles for imposition of duties in advance of importation. When the Bureau decides to change established classification practice, it publishes in the Federal Register its intent to do so. Thirty days are allowed for interested parties to submit any relevant data, views or arguments pertaining to the correct classification. If the Bureau persists in its desire to alter the classification, a Treasury decision is issued, making the new classification effective within 90 days. The following are typical of the hundreds of decisions made under this procedure during 1958:

Item	Old Classification and Rate	New Classification and Rate
Woven labels, chief value of silk........	articles made from fabrics with fast edges @ 19%	manufactures in chief value of silk @ 27½%
Woven labels, chief value of synthetic textile............	articles made from fabrics with fast edges @ 25¢/lb. and 19%	manufactures in chief value of rayon or other synthetic textile, nspf, @ 25¢/lb. and 30%
Coordinate plotters....	drawing instruments @ 19%	mathematical instruments wholly or in chief value of metal, nspf, @ 25½%
Cast iron wing nuts...	castings of iron @ 0.3¢/lb.	castings of iron machined, but not made up into articles @ 5% if non-malleable; nuts of which metal is the component material in chief value if malleable.
Steel wire combs......	articles of metal for manufacture of jewelry, etc. @ 40%	articles designed to be worn on apparel @ 19% to 55%, depending on value.

As illustrated by the preceding examples, the administrative problems of classification go back to the structure of the tariff. Classifications must be made under the stipulations and language drafted by Congress in 1930 which did not foresee technological changes and development of new materials, products and uses. The results are haphazard and shifting. For this reason, importers frequently protest the classification of goods to the Customs Court, even though the process is extremely time-consuming and may involve stiff legal fees. In this manner, radar equipment was first classified as a measuring device and later, as a result of a court decision, acquired the tariff rate of electrical instruments. Uncertainty as to classification is today largely a product of the decisions of the Customs Court.

The large and growing volume of litigation with respect to the classification of merchandise, arising from protests by both importers and domestic producers, can be appreciated from the data in Table 10. It is estimated that some five percent of all dutiable imports are appealed to the courts. This figure takes on added importance by the fact that one court decision may apply to similar articles and thus affect hundreds of entries.

31

TABLE 10

Tariff Classification Cases, U.S. Customs Court, Selected Fiscal Years 1952 to 1959

Year	Cases Pending Beginning of Year	Cases Received During Year	Cases Decided During Year	Cases Pending Close of Year
1952...............	75,109	14,205	6,322	82,992
1954...............	93,503	21,355	13,020	101,874
1956...............	119,285	32,131	19,902	131,567
1958...............	136,306	24,999	38,478	122,875
1959...............	122,875	33,829	26,094	130,610

Source: Administrative Office of the U.S. Courts, *Annual Report of the Director*, Washington, D.C.

The final step in clearing goods through customs is notice of liquidation. The importer is informed as to a rate or amount of duty higher than or lower than that at which his goods were entered. If a lesser amount of duty is due on the goods than was deposited at the time of their entry, the excess is refunded without any claim for refund or other action upon the part of the importer.

CONSOLIDATION AND REVISION OF TARIFF SCHEDULES. The Tariff Commission is currently making a survey of classifications and tariff rates, as directed by the Customs Simplification Act, which will attempt to achieve the following objectives:

• To establish schedules of tariff classifications which will be logical in arrangement and terminology and adapted to the changes which have occurred since 1930, with regard to the character and importance of articles produced in and imported into the United States, and in the markets in which they are sold;

• To eliminate anomalies and illogical results in the classification of articles;

• To simplify the determination and application of tariff classifications.

Although the objective is neither compression nor expansion of the schedule, but clarity, many new items have been specifically included—such as fish sticks, margarine, and instant coffee.

The Commission proposes to consolidate and rearrange the 15 schedules and the Free List now in the Tariff Act into eight new schedules. All of the proposed schedules have now been published. After public hearings have been completed on them, a final draft will be submitted to the President and Congress for consideration. The task was to have been completed by January 1, 1959; however, an indefinite extension has been granted by Congress to allow the Tariff Commission more time. Under the authorizing legislation, Congress must pass a law approving whatever recommendations the Commission submits to it before the proposed consolidated and re-arranged schedules may become effective.

As far as the vast majority of dutiable articles is concerned, this revision does not involve a change in the rate of duty. However, many similar items carrying different tariff rates are grouped together and given a representative rate. One changed definition, in the case of tissue paper, has resulted in a 100 percent increase in the rate of duty for certain papers. In another case, that of chinaware, the Commission had proposed that classification be based on the weight rather than the diameter of dishes. Each plate must now be separately measured to find the aggregate tariff on a set of china. This change was protested in hearings and the original tariff classification was maintained. The significance of these examples is that no change in tariff classifications can be 100 percent neutral with regard to the over-all level of duties.

Marking to Indicate the Country of Origin

The Tariff Act provides that each imported article produced abroad must be legibly marked in a conspicuous place with the name of the country of origin in English. Under authority granted by the Customs Simplification Act, the Treasury Department has abolished this requirement in certain "hardship" cases. Special marking requirements, on the other hand, are specified for a long list of items, including knives, razors, cutlery of all kinds, surgical and dental instruments, watches and clocks. These may involve expensive processes, such as countersinking in the case of sheet glass and iron and steel products. In the case of hypodermic needles and watch bearings, they may be virtually impossible to carry out, while in the case of specialty items, such as dice, marking may seriously damage the merchandise.

Other provisions regarding marking, such as those applicable to wool products, fur products, and containers of alcoholic beverages, are scattered throughout the U.S. Code. In many cases, their effect is to subject foreign products to special requirements which are not applied to domestic products. For instance, the Federal Seed Act requires that imported alfalfa and red clover seed be stained to show its origin.

The chief problem appears to be that an importer may sometimes be unaware, when he does not make specific inquiry to customs in advance, of what will be accepted as a proper country designation or method of marking. This point is best illustrated by the following examples of unsatisfactory marking during recent months given by the Bureau:

Instruction manuals accompanying sewing machines. Such manuals are regarded as separate articles, and accordingly they must be properly marked to show country of origin.

Tuna and other products in cans. If such articles are to be labeled or relabeled after importation, the country of origin of the contents must be legibly and conspicuously marked on a surface of the can where the marking will remain fully visible after the labels are affixed in the United States.

Baseball gloves and mitts. Some were marked by ink stamping inside the glove, or marked by means of a cloth label sewn on the inner side of the strap. No baseball glove or mitt is passed unless the marking is reasonably permanent and is plainly visible upon casual inspection.

Copper pipes and tubes. On April 10, 1958, the Collector of Customs at New York informed importers that the marking requirements with respect to metal articles not specifically included in the list of excepted articles issued under section 304 (a) (3) (J) will be enforced strictly. Each piece of copper pipe and each piece of copper tube must be marked.

Alcoholic beverages. The legend "Bottled and Shipped by John Doe, London, England" alone on a label does not satisfy the requirements, because it does not necessarily indicate the country of origin. In an earlier case, the Customs Court had ruled that diamonds mined in South Africa and cut in Holland should be labeled "Holland".

Pocket knives. A shipment bearing the manufacturer's name on one side of the blade and the country of origin on the other was refused entry. Markings must be on the same side and on the tang of the blade and one below the other.

To take into account the marking requirements of states, as well as of the Federal Government, would swell the list almost endlessly. Arizona and Idaho insist that imported meat and butter be labeled to show country of origin and date of export. Many states require special marking of pillows and mattresses. In South Carolina, retail outlets for imported textiles are required to display a sign to that effect.

In addition to the cost and difficulty of marking, and of the uncertainty as to whether a given mark will pass customs inspection, a third problem arises as to what to do with rejected shipments. Articles may not always be re-marked and imported without penalty. Sometimes they must be re-exported; in other cases, improper marking is subject to a fine even where the improper marking was unintentional. Compensation and expenses of customs officials assigned to supervise the exportation, destruction or re-marking of improperly marked articles and containers are borne by the importer.

Laws Against Unfair Competitive Practices

A number of apparently overlapping provisions of law, ostensibly designed to suppress unethical business practices in international trade, lend themselves to other ulterior motives. As a purely hypothetical illustration, let us suppose that a producer of cherries in the State of Washington discovers that a Canadian cherry producer is just about to make a shipment of cherries to the United States—beautifully ripe cherries, ready for the market. The domestic grower proceeds forthwith to put in a dumping complaint, or a complaint that they were sold by unfair methods, or that they were picked by convict labour. While the case is being investigated, the cherries remain unshipped, and rot. The case is dismissed on a determination that the charge is untrue. Despite the very real financial loss suffered, neither the prospective U.S. importer of the cherries nor the Canadian exporter can obtain any redress.

The most general part of the U.S. laws relating to unfair import practices, Section 337 of the Tariff Act, provides for import restrictions on goods which are found to have been imported or sold by "unfair methods". Provision is made for study by the Tariff Commission, since injury to a domestic industry must be established. Pending completion of the investigation, the President may restrict imports by requiring posting of a bond. If a violation of the Act is found, the goods must be either exported or destroyed or the bond is forfeited.

This section (and its predecessor, section 316 of the Tariff Act of 1922), has been enforced in cases involving patent and trade-mark infringement, copying of distinctive nonfunctional features of American goods, and imitating distinctive packaging of American goods.

Section 307 of the Tariff Act prohibits imports of goods produced with the use of convict labour. In addition, the section contains a prohibition on importation of goods produced abroad by forced or indentured labour, with the qualification that such goods may be imported if they are not "mined, produced, or manufactured in such quantities in the United States as to meet the consumptive demands of the United States."

Sections 1124 and 1125 of Title 15 of the U.S. Code prohibit entry of foreign goods bearing infringements of registered trade-marks or goods which are falsely marked to indicate a place of production other than their true origin. Section 106 of Title 17 prohibits entry of pirated copies of copyrighted books. The history of the administration of these sections provides instances in which the customs confiscated shipments because some U.S. firms had bought the "American rights" to well-known foreign brand names. Although the private interest of the U.S. firm is clear, it is not so evident that the public interest is served by invoking the power of the government to exclude all imports of the original product, when labeled, into the United States.

The Antidumping Act is the most widely-known of these laws. It provides that when the Secretary of the Treasury determines that a class or kind of foreign merchandise is being, or is likely to be sold to purchasers in the United States at less than its fair value, he shall so advise the Tariff Commission. The Commission shall determine whether an industry in the United

States is being or is likely to be injured, or is prevented from being established, by reason of the importation of such merchandise. If the determination is in the affirmative—a tie vote being considered an affirmative vote—the Secretary must make public a finding of dumping. There is no provision for Presidential review of dumping findings.

There are, of course, a large number of complex technical problems involved in these procedures. The law provides a number of alternate bases for determining "fair value". In the case of investigations by the Tariff Commission, the law does not define either "industry" or "injury". Obviously, there is much leeway for human judgment in dumping cases. Customs officers must, and other citizens may, report suspected dumping.

The determination as to whether merchandise is being sold to purchasers in the United States at less than fair value is ordinarily based upon a comparison between the net, f.o.b. factory price to U.S. importers and the net, f.o.b. factory price to purchasers in home market. However, a large number of factors—such as quantity discounts, advertising costs, commissions, and the like—may make the investigation a difficult one. No publicity is given to such investigations; the first notice would be publication in the Federal Register of an order to withhold appraisement of a certain type of merchandise. This order is made retroactive to merchandise which entered up to 120 days before the complaint was received.

Although these procedures hold a constant threat over the importer's head, the total number of cases is small. During 1958, only 36 complaints of dumping were received by the Bureau, 22 foreign investigations were made, and two determinations of sale at less than fair value were issued.[1] Some 40 cases are currently being considered. Over the past four years, of more than 100 cases given serious study by the Treasury, 12 decisions were referred to the Tariff Commission. The result has been one injury determination, in the case of cast iron soil pipe and 11 no-injury decisions, in the case of potash (three countries), pencil sharpeners, nicotine sulfate, montan wax (two countries), hardboard (two countries), and tissue paper (two countries).

Injury determinations by the Tariff Commission border on the capricious. In the soil pipe case, the decision was based on the fact that there was one marginal producer in the country who was injured by imports equal to under four-tenths of one percent of domestic production. This producer had not been making a profit even when there had been no imports, and had closed down on three previous occasions within 20 years; in addition over-all production and prices had been rising. In the tissue paper case,

---

1. In the spring of 1959, appraisement was withheld on welded pipe and tubing and on birch doors originating in Canada. The Treasury subsequently ruled that these items "[were] not being nor [were] likely to be sold at less than fair value".

imports were found to be about three percent of U.S. consumption, but the determination of no injury appeared to hinge upon lack of "predatory intent".

In case of injury determination, the Secretary of the Treasury must make a finding of dumping and order appraisers of merchandise to assess a dumping duty based on the difference between U.S. and home market prices. The damage to importers is likely to be withholding of appraisement prior to the finding of dumping rather than the dumping duty itself.

Health and Quarantine Restrictions

"A spice supplier in a foreign country sought to establish trade with the United States. To his dismay his first shipments were rejected by the United States pure food authorities at port of entry. Something was said about filth and insanitary conditions. A foreign manufacturer of a medicinal preparation learned, too late to save the expense of shipment to the United States, that it was barred from entry because it was a 'new drug'. A foreign cosmetic manufacturer, planning business with American importers, heard rumors that the United States Government imposes restrictions on the dyes that may be used in such products."[1]

A number of legal provisions govern such matters as standards of identity, purity and quality, in the case of foods; directions for use, adequate warnings and recognition by medical experts as being safe for the intended use, in the case of drugs and instruments intended for medical use; and statements of quantity and warnings as to possible injurious effects, in the case of cosmetics and other products. In the majority of cases, these regulations apply alike to domestic and imported goods. However, they have a number of effects which foreign exporters consider unwarranted.

Even experienced importers dealing in specific commodities are constantly surprised by the applications of administrative standards, for the standards which some products must pass are not specified. A shipment can be detained if the container is considered too big for its contents (and therefore misleading), even if the net weight is listed on the outside—as in the case of a European chocolate manufacturer. The fact that a shipment may have slipped by because of limited facilities for inspection will not insure the admission of a subsequent shipment which does not comply fully with the law; nor will it exempt any shipment from possible later action under the "domestic" provisions of the Food, Drug and Cosmetic Act.

One-sixth to one-tenth of all shipments sampled are withheld. This is a clear indication of the stringency of the standards. Among the products detained during recent months, the following are typical:

---

1. U.S. Department of Health, Education and Welfare, "Requirements of the United States Food, Drug and Cosmetic Act", U.S. Government Printing Office, 1958 Rev., page v.

Sugar candy—common or usual names of all ingredients not given and artificial color not declared;

Canned vegetables—net contents not in terms of avoirdupois units;

Medicinal preparations—prescription items are not safe for use except under supervision of a physician;

Canned mushrooms—label declares "French Mushrooms", whereas it is a product of Japan.

A cosmetic (except a hair dye) may contain only coal-tar colours which come from a batch tested by the Food and Drug Administration and certified as being harmless for the intended use. In practice, the colours used in these and other products must sometimes be purchased in the United States in order to pass inspection.

In addition to general standards of purity and quality, imported plants and animals, and foodstuffs derived from plants and animals, are subject to the special measures for preventing the spread of plant and animal diseases which are administered by the U.S. Department of Agriculture. Fresh fruits and vegetables and meat for human consumption are not inspected at the Canadian border by Agriculture officials. However, all live animals and certain types of plant material must enter the United States at designated quarantine stations, of which there are some 69 in all. Some stations are at border points separated by more than 300 air miles. This doubtless involves hardship on a few isolated communities, but hardly qualifies as a major barrier to trade. Importers of live animals must produce a certificate signed by a salaried veterinarian of the Canadian Government, certifying that they are free of specified diseases and have not been exposed for 60 days prior to export. Tuberculin and Brucellosis test or vaccination certificates are required for cattle.

Potatoes from Newfoundland and fresh corn from Manitoba west to the Pacific are embargoed. Elm trees, and lumber and boxes, crates, etc. made of elm lumber with bark, are prohibited from Quebec, but can be imported from other parts of Canada. Black currants from any part of Canada are embargoed. These regulations are frequently reviewed by competent technicians, and it appears fair to say that Federal animal and plant quarantine regulations respecting Canada are at a bare minimum. There is close cooperation on a working level between personnel of the two governments.

State and local sanitary and quarantine regulations are another matter, however. These are sometimes more severe than those of the Federal Government, and often assume a protectionist tinge. The heterogenity of state and local regulations and excessive delay in lifting quarantines are frequently criticized. New York state provides that only fluid milk which has been inspected and approved by state authorities can be sold in the state. These authorities will not send their inspectors to Canada.[1] California imposes an outright embargo on Canadian sheep, many fresh fruits and vegetables and certain types of nursery stock.

One procedural change which has been repeatedly urged is the assignment of inspectors by the Food and Drug Administration and the Department of Agriculture to the pier or terminal to examine each incoming shipment in order to avoid its being unloaded and held in bond at a warehouse. The need for some measure of coordination between state and Federal health and quarantine regulations, and for reciprocal agreements between states on these points, has also been stressed. This is an extremely difficult area of public policy, and one where the economic issues, as well as the scientific, medical, and constitutional problems involved, should be given greater consideration.

Government Purchasing

Government procurement officials must observe numerous provisions of Federal law requiring preference to be given to U.S. goods. For instance, the current appropriations act for the national military establishment (P.L. 85-724, August, 1958) specifies that preference must be given to domestic food, clothing, silk yarn and wool grown or processed in the United States. No percentage margin is laid down as to the preferences which must be granted under this law. The Defense Department may take into account various criteria, including strategic and logistic considerations, or whether the domestic industry in question is a "small business" or is in an economically depressed or a surplus labour area.[2]

A more general law, the Buy American Act, lays down the principle that only goods produced in the United States shall be bought for public use. Purchasing officials may buy goods of foreign origin only when:
 • the purchase of domestic goods is inconsistent with the public interest; or
 • the goods are not produced in the United States in sufficient and reasonably available commercial quantities and of a satisfactory quality; or
 • the cost of the goods is unreasonable; or
 • the goods are to be used outside the United States.

The President has, by executive order, established two alternative rules for defining the degree of preference established under the Buy American Act. The first of these is a preference of six percent of the bid or offered price of materials of foreign origin, including duty. The second is a preference of 10 percent of the bid or offered price of the foreign goods, not including duty or other costs incurred after arrival in the United States.[3]

---

1. Senate of Canada, Proceedings of the Standing Committee on Canadian Trade Relations, No. 5, 1948, page 99.

2. Defense Department Directive 4105.22, June, 1952.

3. Executive Order 10582, December 17, 1954.

In several important respects, these arithmetical limits on the permissible margin between domestic and foreign prices are not significant. On the one hand, a "handicap" of up to 12 percent may be granted to small business and to business in areas of substantial unemployment, as determined by the Secretary of Labor. To accept a domestic bid when it is more than 12 percent above the foreign bid, the buying agency may fall back upon national security considerations. Thus any foreign bid may be rejected upon receipt of advice from the Office of Civil and Defense Mobilization that "essential national security interests" may be involved.

On the other hand, numerous exceptions and waivers have been applied. The three U.S. Armed Services have relaxed their restrictions on Canadian procurement. Each service has published a broad list of products—such as "weapons", "motor vehicles", "ammunition and explosives", "aircraft", "communication equipment", "photographic equipment", "maintenance and repair shop equipment", etc.—for which the Buy American Act is waived in respect to Canadian bids on proposals for prime contracts. In addition to the items listed by the Armed Services as exempt in regard to Canadian suppliers only, there is a long list of articles, materials and supplies which are exempt from all restrictions of the Buy American Act, provided they do not originate from certain prescribed areas of the world. In the case of subcontracts for listed products, the Canadian goods are to be considered as U.S. material. Thus, a U.S. defense contractor can theoretically buy anything up to 100 percent of his products from a Canadian source.

If a U.S. prime contractor is producing an unlisted product, he must keep the entire Canadian or foreign content below 50 percent unless the Armed Service is willing to waive this stipulation. A similar list of excepted items applies to Canadian materials used in construction projects. Finally, it should be recalled that the Buy American Act relates to physical materials and is not concerned with contracts where the supplier delivers a service—such as findings resulting from a research and development contract.

Defense items account for over 80 percent of Federal Government procurements. Protests of interested governments sometimes bring to light questionable cases in other areas, such as four rejections of electrical generating equipment with up to $875,130 difference between individual domestic and overseas bids in each case. The Post Office Department's chief purchasing agent was recently quoted as saying that he would have nothing to do with foreign business machines "regardless of any price differential, whether 6 or 50 percent".[1]

---

1. *The Journal of Commerce*, New York, December 23, 1958. In July 1959, the ban against foreign-made office machines and equipment for post offices throughout the country was lifted. However, "by avoiding any mention of relative prices . . . and emphasizing that full consideration be given to available repair and service facilities, the department appears to be de-emphasizing the factor most favorable to imports and re-emphasizing the factor that could be most favorable to domestic machines". (*The Journal of Commerce*, New York, August 5, 1959.)

In addition to the Buy American Act and the appropriations act cited, similar "Buy American" provisions appear in the Merchant Marine Act, the Rural Electrification Act, the Strategic and Critical Materials Stockpiling Act, and in Federal housing legislation. Four states also have Buy American legislation governing all public procurement.[2]

"Buy American" provisions for Federal construction and Federal-aid highway work are outlined as follows by the Bureau of Public Roads:

- The bidder must indicate in his bid whether he proposes to furnish a foreign article or material;

- The bid price shall include applicable duty;

- For the purpose of comparing bids, the total bid price *on the entire contract submitted by any bidder offering a material or articles of foreign origin* shall be increased by an amount equal to six percent of the bid price for such material or article;

- The contract shall be based upon the bid as submitted, without regard to such differential.

On January 1, 1960, these uniform requirements superseded more restrictive state regulations formerly in effect.

The Defense Amendment

It was not until 1954 that a need was felt to control imports to prevent impairment of the industrial mobilization base of the United States. The 1954 Trade Agreements Extension Act was broadened the following year to grant additional authority to the President in controlling imports for security reasons:

It would appear that under the new (1955) amendment the President can, on account of security considerations, impose new or increased tariff duties on imports, without any limitation as to their level, or he can impose an import quota, so as to reduce imports to such levels as he deems appropriate. The only limitation on the President's authority to control imports under this amendment is that his action must be such "as he deems necessary to adjust the imports of such article to a level that will not threaten to impair the national security".[1]

---

2. California's attorney general has ruled that the Buy American law of that state is superseded by U.S. treaty clauses specifying Most-Favoured-Nation treatment for the goods of other countries.

1. Report to the Committee on Ways and Means on United States Customs, Tariff and Trade Agreement Laws and Their Administration from the Subcommittee on Customs, Tariffs and Reciprocal Trade Agreements, Government Printing Office, Washington, D.C., 1957, page 100.

The date and abrupt manner in which Congress introduced this new principle in U.S. commercial policy cause one to wonder whether national defense is the sole reason for the so-called "defense amendment". Why was it not introduced during World War II or the Korean War?

The Congress made a further effort to spell out its intent in the Trade Agreements Extension Act of 1958. Factors which the Director of the Office of Civil and Defense Mobilization may take into account in deciding whether imports of any particular article might constitute a threat to national security were thereby enumerated as follows:

(1) domestic production needed for defense requirements, "including restoration and rehabilation";

(2) the capacity of industries to meet such requirements, taking into account all pertinent economic factors;

(3) the "requirements of growth" of domestic industries;

(4) the over-all effect that imported commodities "have or will have on such industries and the capacity of the United States to meet national security requirements";

(5) the "economic welfare" of the nation "as it is related to our national security, including the impact of foreign competition on the economic welfare of individual domestic industries".

In each case, the OCDM Director must make public his decision whether to recommend import curbs to the President. In some cases, public hearings may be held to obtain further information, and notice of these hearings are published in the Federal Register. Procedures to be followed in requesting an investigation were first issued by OCDM on January 15, 1958, four years after the initial "defense amendment" was passed.

The OCDM Director and the House Ways and Means Committee have stressed the point that the national security amendment is not a substitute for the more general Trade Agreements escape clause. In its report on the Trade Agreements Extension Act of 1958, the House Ways and Means Committee said:

Your committee was guided by the view that the national security amendment is not an alternative to the means afforded by the escape clause for providing industries which believe themselves injured a second court in which to seek relief. Its purpose is a different one—to provide those best able to judge national security needs, namely, the President and the Director of the Office of Defense Mobilization, acting with the advice of such Cabinet officers as the Secretaries of Defense, Commerce and State, a way of taking whatever action is needed to avoid a threat to the national security through imports. Serious injury to a particular industry, which is the principal consideration in the escape clause procedure, may also be a consideration bearing on the national security position in particular cases, but the avoidance or remedy of injury to industries is not the object per se.

Apparently the House Ways and Means Committee has every intention of backing the policy it set forth in this report. Some time in the near future, the House Ways and Means Subcommittee on Trade Policy plans to summon respective Administrative agency spokesmen to explain their use of the security and defense arguments in imposing import controls. The Subcommittee is particularly interested in the Greer's Ferry affair, in which a contract for turbines for the Arkansas project was awarded to a U.S. firm, on security grounds, despite a foreign bid that was 20 percent, or $300,000 lower. Criticism of the award was particularly strong, as the British bid was ignored in the wake of a budget message from the President stressing the desirability of thrift in the spending of U.S. funds. On the more general issue of why national security becomes the excuse for import curbs, the Subcommittee is expected to ask for specific details concerning defense factors considered by the OCDM in deciding whether to urge the President to curb imports as a means of bolstering defensive strength.

The defense amendment has set in motion a number of complex and time-consuming investigations, involving highly controversial issues. The OCDM has emphasized that even when decisions on cases have been reached and announced, they cannot always be regarded as final. In the event that new information should become available or circumstances regarding the issue should change, the OCDM will reopen its investigations.

Six cases are currently under active consideration by OCDM:

(1) *Steam turbines.* Westinghouse and General Electric filed a petition to cover steam turbines in February 1959. The petition was filed separately to avoid delay on the anticipated OCDM ruling on the four other categories of heavy electrical generating equipment.[1] Their immediate purpose is to obtain an OCDM ruling under Section 3(d) of Executive Order 10582 to advise Tennessee Valley Authority to cancel its order for a steam turbine-generator unit from C.A. Parsons Ltd., a British firm. Both petitions maintain that the steam turbine plants of all three domestic producers of this type of equipment are located in cities classified as "areas of substantial unemployment" and "areas of substantial labour surplus" under OCDM Defense Manpower Policy No. 4 and Executive Order 10582.

The Tennessee Valley Authority (TVA) has reacted strongly to the General Electric-Westinghouse campaign to overturn its award. TVA announced in its bid instructions that a foreign bid had to be at least 20 percent below the nearest domestic bid to qualify. Parsons, with its $12.1 million offer, was

---

1. It was subsequently ruled that these other categories of equipment may be imported without affecting national security.

$5.5 million, or more than 30 percent below the General Electric and Westinghouse bids, which were approximately equal.

In a memorandum circulated to inquiring Congressmen, the TVA board of directors criticized the American power equipment industry and challenged the industry's claim that U.S. national defense requires competitive imports to be banned. The memorandum said that since 1951, the prices charged for such equipment have increased more than 50 percent, while the average wholesale price of all commodities has increased only about five percent. However, TVA also stated that even if General Electric or Westinghouse had bid lower than Parson's, they would not have been awarded the contract because both their bids were "unresponsive and unacceptable".

The briefs submitted by General Electric and Westinghouse requested OCDM to advise TVA to cancel its contract with Parsons on or before March 9, 1959, but investigation is still in progress.

(2) *Tankers carrying petroleum.* In September 1959, the Joint Commission for American Flag Tankers filed a petition to require half of all U.S. petroleum and petroleum products imports to be carried in U.S. bottoms, or to give import quotas to individual U.S. tanker operators.

(3) *Wool knit gloves.* A petition was filed in February 1959 by the OCDM Director without a formal request from the domestic industry. Additional information has been requested from three domestic manufacturing associations to bring up to date the material they submitted to OCDM during the wool fabrics investigation.

(4) *Surplus military rifles.* Application for investigation was made on June 29, 1959, by the Sporting Arms and Ammunition Manufacturers' Institute on behalf of six domestic manufacturers of sporting firearms: High Standard Manufacturing Corporation, Ithaca Gun Company, O.F. Mossberg and Sons, Inc., Remington Arms Company, Inc., Savage Arms Corporation and the Winchester Division of Olin Mathieson Chemical Corporation. The investigation does not involve ordinary commercial imports of sporting firearms but is restricted to foreign surplus military rifles imported into the United States for sale as sporting arms.

(5) *Transistors and related electronic products.* In September 1959, the Electronics Industries Association petitioned for import curbs on all semiconductor products, including diodes, rectifiers and transistors imported as separate units or contained in finished products.

(6) *Dental burrs.* The American Dental Trade Association of Washington, D.C. originally filed a petition under Section 7 of the Trade Agreements Act in May 1957, withdrew their application in August 1957, and re-filed it in May 1958. The industry group met with OCDM in December 1958, and although OCDM indicated that the petition would probably be denied, the group insisted upon having an investigation conducted. Except for a

few scattered protests from dental practitioners against the application, little interest has been shown in the case thus far.

The OCDM, in recent decisions, has established that imports of the following do not constitute a threat to the national security: wool, cotton and rayon textiles; jeweled and pin-lever watches; hard-fiber farm and industrial cordage; fluorspar; cobalt; and hydraulic turbine-driven generators, transformers and power circuit breakers. In announcing this last decision, OCDM asked Federal procurement agencies to consider requiring contractors to have facilities on this continent to service the equipment supplied. The most important decision under the defense amendment to date involves the imposition of mandatory import controls on crude oil and the principal petroleum derivatives. This decision was subsequently amended to exclude oil imports via pipeline, motor carrier or rail from the country in which they were produced.

No final conclusion can be made as to the degree to which the defense amendment constitutes a barrier to trade with Canada. The few cases that the OCDM has so far decided do not provide a sufficient basis for judgment. But the threat of the defense amendment as a trade barrier is apparent. Despite the OCDM Director's assurance that the defense amendment provisions would not serve as a further court of appeal for firms failing to obtain relief under escape clause action, two investigations of cases presented to OCDM are being postponed until the firms discover whether they are able to limit imports under the escape clause. If appeals to the Tariff Commission fail, the OCDM will resume its investigations. Another example concerns the petition recently filed to restrict imports of transistors and other commercial radio components. Prior to the filing of the petition, it was reported that the spokesman for the group said that one reason the manufacturers chose to go to OCDM for import relief was because of the meager record of successful industry applications for import relief to the Tariff Commission under the escape clause provision.[1]

The "Invisible Tariff"

There can be little doubt that the regulations and procedures outlined in the preceding pages constitute barriers to trade. The U.S. laws contain many loopholes through which domestic firms can harass their foreign competitors. The additional barriers thus established strongly reinforce the structure of tariffs and quotas.

Although its effects are evident in many lines of business, the "invisible tariff" is perhaps felt most strongly in the area of manufactured consumers' goods. Delays occasioned by valuation and classification procedures are most likely to hinder trade in those items where style and model changes are an important factor. Restrictive sanitary and marking regulations are

---

1. *The Journal of Commerce*, New York, February 23, 1959.

likely to add significantly to production costs of low-priced goods. With regard to intermediate products, there have been instances of workmen refusing to handle or process materials made abroad.

In considering proposals for reform, the nature of administrative procedures in this area must be carefully analyzed. Certain activities involve only the observance of a pervasive set of legislative provisions. Other activities provide numerous opportunities for administrators to exercise discretion. Valuation and classification, although guided by a detailed body of administrative regulations, remain closely circumscribed by customs law. In only one sense can their administration be considered dynamic—domestic business firms are permitted to protest the rulings of the Customs Bureau. This procedure provides opportunities for obtaining rulings which would have the effect of raising their competitors' taxes, of increasing their competitors' costs of doing business, or, in some cases, of making their competitors' product less attractive in U.S. markets. When the rather considerable administrative recourses have been exhausted, the U.S. firms may in some cases then commence lawsuits in the Customs Court to accomplish these same purposes.

Not only do these efforts frequently succeed in the first instance, but also the domestic firm may gain a strong competitive advantage in the future. Judicial interpretations have all too often compelled alterations of marketing arrangements and tax structure at home and abroad in directions which are not closely related to commercial practice. The economic facts and issues involved in customs procedures are therefore badly in need of definition and analysis.

In two other vital areas, the suppression of unfair business practices and the control of goods injurious to health and morals, much greater opportunity exists for administrative discretion. The record shows that administration of the antidumping and patent and trade-mark laws has been restrained and has not resulted in widespread harassment of importers. There have been few investigations of dumping and fewer still of trade-mark infringement.

Marking requirements may also be altered by the Customs Bureau, but there has not been much noticeable liberalization in recent years. These areas of wider administrative discretion bear watching lest in the future a protectionist administration should look upon these policing activities as fortuitous vehicles for greatly increasing protection for U.S. producers from foreign competition.

5

Canadian Administrative Protectionism

IN CANADA, the bulk of the administrative barriers are related to one of four matters—tariff classification, valuation for duty, liquidation and litigation, or trade restrictions arising entirely outside the tariff system. Such barriers can be a most severe type of protection, a possibility which prompted B. A. Levett to state "Let me write the Administration Act and I care not who writes the rates of duty".[1]

The Legal and Administrative Framework

The Canadian tariff is administered under the Customs Act, the Customs Tariff Act, the Tariff Board Act, and other Federal statutes. The Department of Finance is primarily responsible for formulating government policy and proposing legislation, and the Department of National Revenue administers the legislation and regulations thereunder. The Tariff Board of Canada acts as an administrative appeal board, deciding on appeals from decisions of the Deputy Minister of National Revenue (Customs Division), and also conducts enquiries and makes reports on matters referred to it by the Minister of Finance. Thus, appeals are handled by essentially administrative procedures in Canada in contrast with the judicial procedures in the United States, and consequently tend to be more expeditiously dealt with.

Canadian customs statutes confer upon the Cabinet as a whole, or upon the Minister of National Revenue, the power to make regulations for certain specific purposes or generally for carrying out the spirit of the legislation. In addition, departmental officials at lower levels have a certain amount of flexibility in making decisions. Thus, considerable discretionary power is given to those administering the tariff, and any attempt to discover how specific imports will be treated must include an examination of not only the statutes but also the relevant orders in council, departmental regulations, memoranda to port collectors, and other departmental communications and rule-of-thumb practices of customs officials.

---

1. Levett, B. A., *Through the Customs Maze*, New York, 1923, page 11.

Classification

One of the most important questions facing an importer is under which of the many tariff items will his goods be classified by the customs officials, and, therefore, what rate of duty must he pay. Although this question can be answered with assurance in the majority of cases, there are many instances when it is not so simple. The Canadian tariff is comprehensive in the sense that every permissible import must be classified under some item in the schedule. Most of the groupings contain a basket item covering all types of the commodity not specified elsewhere, and item 711 is an overall "basket item", providing rates of BP 15 percent and MFN 20 percent.

SECTION 50 OF THE CUSTOMS ACT. This section states that if an article is enumerated in the customs tariff under two or more items, the item with the highest rate of duty shall be applicable. In other words, the benefit of the doubt is not given in favor of the importer. Due to the complexity of the Canadian tariff and the piecemeal fashion in which it has developed to cover different commodities, it is easy to see how an imported article could enter Canada under more than one tariff item. When such a situation occurs, the importer may well be surprised when he is charged a higher rate than he had anticipated.

MADE-IN-CANADA RULINGS. In some cases, the Canadian tariff prescribes one rate of duty for an article if it is "of a class or kind made in Canada" and a lower rate if it is "of a class or kind not made in Canada". One very good example is that of the machinery items 427 and 427a, which bear MFN rates of 22½ percent and 7½ percent respectively, depending on whether the article of machinery is of a class or kind made in Canada.[1]

The Tariff Act provides that for goods to be considered of a class or kind made in Canada, they must be produced in substantial quantities. The Cabinet shall determine what percentage of the normal Canadian consumption shall be considered "substantial". Since 1936, this percentage has remained at 10 percent. It remains a most difficult classification distinction to administer, the decision in many cases depending on whether the words "class or kind" are taken to refer to a wide or to a narrow range of goods. This fact leaves a good deal of discretion in the hands of customs officials. For example, a particular type of rifle might be of a class or kind not made in Canada if only that type is considered, but of a class or kind made in Canada if all types of rifles are considered.

Sometimes rather peculiar results come from these "made-in-Canada" regulations. Silk and artificial silk fabrics of a class or kind not made in Canada, when used in the manufacture of neckties, scarves or mufflers, come in at MFN 15 percent. The Department of National Revenue has ruled that some types of fabrics which are made in Canada are suitable for

---

1. See "Industrial Machinery," page 90.

scarves and mufflers, but not for neckties. Thus, a particular fabric import may be deemed of a class or kind not made in Canada when used in the manufacture of neckties, but of a class or kind made in Canada when used for scarves and mufflers.

These "made-in-Canada" rulings have unquestionably been a burden both to the importer and to the customs administration. Many decisions have been appealed to the Tariff Board, and in one case concerning machinery imports, the Board stated, "Indeed it is difficult to conceive any precise terms which would be suitable for differentiating the various and differing 'machinery' dutiable under tariff items 427 and 427a."[1] In addition, the importer faces the possibility that goods now entering as "not made in Canada" may be reclassified to "made in Canada" with only three weeks' notice of change required.

In his 1959 Budget, the Minister of Finance pointed out that:

with the increasing complexity and variety of modern machines, these "class or kind" provisions create uncertainties. Much time and expense are involved in trying to clarify "class or kind" questions before the courts.

He then went on to remove any future uncertainty concerning six types of machinery by introducing them specifically into the tariff schedule under item 427, which is the higher rate. These types of machinery had been especially troublesome to classify in the past, and had all been ruled to be of a class or kind made in Canada, so that no change in rates was involved. The six categories include certain types of fork-lift trucks, power shovels and cranes, paper machines, and electrical generating sets.

The customs administration has a regulation dealing with the machinery items which states that unless the imported machinery has been ruled by the Department to be of a class or kind not made in Canada, customs entries are to be entered as "made in Canada". This regulation seems to be at variance with an important decision by the Supreme Court of Canada in the Dominion Engineering Works case handed down in October 1958, which stated that it is impossible to hold that Parliament intended to give greater weight to one tariff item than another.

END-USE ITEMS. The Canadian tariff abounds in end-use or specific-use items, which reduce the duty on certain articles if they are to be used for a specific purpose in Canada, usually in the manufacture of specific commodities. In this way, different rates are levied against many articles, depending on what they are used for. The abundance of these items contributes a good deal to the multiplicity of rates and the complexities of the tariff, but despite the administrative problems, the device is such a flexible method of providing specialized tariff relief that the end-use items continue to grow in number.

---

1. A-260, T.B.C. 272, March 18, 1953.

It should be pointed out, however, that efforts toward eliminating end-use items have been made recently. In the summer of 1958, the primary iron and steel sector of the tariff was completely overhauled and simplified, with a great many end-use items being eliminated.

Many of the reductions in duty paid on articles used for a specific purpose take the form not of lower tariff rates, but of drawbacks or remissions of duty paid, as set down in Schedule B of the Tariff. These drawbacks usually are 99 percent of the duty paid (excluding any dumping duty), as in the case of bituminous coal "when imported by proprietors of coke ovens and converted at their coke ovens into coke for use in the smelting of metals from ores and in the melting of metals".

These end-use items sometimes occasion extra costs for the importer in determining just what the goods are used for. For example, cotton lace and embroidery bear a lower rate when used by manufacturers than when consumed directly at the retail level, and importers selling mainly to manufacturing firms but also to retail outlets must keep special records showing the proportion of each import shipment which was subsequently sold to each class of buyer. They are allowed to pay the lower rate at the time of entry, and then must submit an amended entry quarterly to cover the extra duty payable arising from their sales to retail outlets.

ORDER IN COUNCIL ITEMS. Section 273 of the Customs Act empowers the Cabinet to reduce by order in council the duty on any article used by Canadian manufacturers. These order in council items are usually based on a specific use and are normally of a temporary nature, although they often become incorporated in the tariff itself as end-use items.

Similarly, the Cabinet may, by order in council, remit all or part of the duty normally payable on particular imports, such action being taken in special situations. In this manner, duties applied to the pipe used to build the Trans-Canada Pipeline and other major pipelines were remitted in part.

COUNTRY OF ORIGIN. As mentioned earlier, goods must be shipped directly from the country of origin if they are to be entered under the British Preference or Most-Favoured-Nation tariff rate. This requirement provides indirect protection to Canadian ocean ports and transportation facilities, frequently by ruling out more economical transportation via U.S. ocean ports and inland railways. The St. Lawrence Seaway, of course, makes direct shipping through Canadian ports more economical and thereby reduces the effective protection afforded by this requirement.

COMMONWEALTH CONTENT PROVISIONS. The idea of British content has been extended in the case of a few tariff items to provide an incentive for Canadian businessmen to manufacture a greater percentage of their product directly in Canada and/or purchase more component parts from Canadian or British Commonwealth suppliers. The best example is the automobile schedule, in which the MFN rate of 17½ percent on certain automobile parts is reduced to free entry, provided a given proportion of the importing manufacturer's materials costs are incurred in the British Commonwealth. For passenger cars, the requirement is 60 percent for manufacturers producing over 20,000 units, which means all the major firms. Since almost no parts are imported from British countries, this British content provision in fact becomes a Canadian content provision. Paradoxically, this is a type of tariff reduction which encourages domestic production, thereby providing yet another barrier to imports from the United States. (The economic implications of these provisions are discussed more fully in Chapter 7.)

COMPONENT PARTS. A large number of tariff disputes concern the treatment of component parts. Should an article be classified as a component part of another article or as a separate entity? For example, a case before the Tariff Board a few years ago concerned the classification of certain tractor covers as either tractor parts (free entry) or as separate textile items (25 percent). The Board ruled that the tractor cover could not be considered a part of a tractor but was in fact a distinct entity. On the other hand, the Board ruled that plastic radio cabinets could be entered as parts of radio receiving sets (27 percent) instead of plastic furniture (27½ percent). When an article is entered in unassembled form, consisting of all and only the parts required to assemble it, it is normally considered an entirety, and classed as a complete set of parts (in most cases, a complete set of parts is dutiable at the same rate as the assembled entirety). However, when parts are entered separately, say as repair parts, certain articles, such as nuts and bolts and ball bearings, must be entered as distinct items, and are dutiable at their specified rate. Such a requirement undoubtedly adds to the cost and trouble of documenting the import entry, and may also unpleasantly surprise the inexperienced importer concerning the rate of duty.

WHOLLY OR IN PART. Many tariff items prescribe rates for an article composed of a certain material. Usually the item covers all articles composed "wholly or in chief part" (by weight or volume, etc.), or "wholly or in chief value" of a particular material, the former criterion being preferable since it is based on physical characteristics which can usually be determined from the article itself at time of entry.

Difficulties in classification sometimes occur when goods are made of several different substances. This is particularly true of many textile items, where such complexities make it difficult for importers of textiles and clothing to estimate beforehand the duty payable. An importer of fabrics from the United States, for example, finds that woven cotton fabrics are divided into three classes according to value, each bearing different rates. Fabrics containing any wool or rayon bear higher compound rates; and other rates are provided for fabrics whose chief weight is silk, or which are composed wholly or in part of vegetable fiber but not containing wool, silk, or synthetic textile fibers. G. A. Elliott comments as follows on these problems:

> It is apparent that importers of garments or textile articles must be provided with a great deal of detailed information in order to classify their imports properly. If an exporter does not provide on his invoice information sufficient to allow the importer to classify the article correctly, delay and additional expense are inevitable. An unexpected thread of wool, for example, not only in the main parts of the garment but in the facing or decoration, may subject the entire article to a different classification. It is not surprising that Canadian importers of textiles and clothing quite generally claim that it is very difficult to forecast the laid-down cost of their imports.[1]

There are a number of other classification difficulties which cause trouble from time to time. These include the treatment of containers, technical and biological distinctions, and simple overlapping and ambiguity. To quote Elliott again, "Is an ash-tray, combined with a music box, an ash-tray or a music box or neither? Doubtless some will be tempted to decide that the producer and importer of such a monstrosity deserve that it be classified in the basket item, which bears the highest of all rates in the tariff".[2]

Thus, problems relating to classification cause uncertainties of one kind or another to importers, and add to their costs, thereby tending to discourage the flow of trade. In particular, they are burdensome in the case of products entering Canada for the first time, or of firms selling to Canada for the first time. For this reason, the development of new trade channels may be delayed or frustrated altogether.[3]

Valuation and Anti-Dumping Duties

An importer is not only concerned with the classification of his goods but also with their valuation for duty purposes. Where the rate is of the

---

1. Elliott, G. A., *Tariff Procedures and Trade Barriers*, University of Toronto Press, 1955, page 65.

2. *Ibid.*, page 97.

3. One Canadian procedure which helps reduce classification uncertainties should be mentioned. It is the pre-import decision. Where an importer is in doubt about the treatment his goods will receive, he may obtain an informal ruling from the Department of National Revenue before bringing the goods into Canada. Such rulings have, with a few exceptions, been quite dependable, and in the odd case where misunderstanding or error has occurred, the Minister has frequently recommended a refund of duty. However, such pre-import decisions may be upset later by a decision of the Tariff Board on an appeal by a domestic competitor. In addition, an appeal may refer only to a particular shipment and does not guarantee that a change in the manner of classification will not occur in the future. Appeals take time to obtain, in themselves adding to the importer's expense, and therefore cannot be requested too frequently, certainly not prior to every shipment.

ad valorem type, the duty he must pay obviously depends on the valuation, along with the level of the rate itself. In addition, any dumping duties which might be levied on the goods depend on their dutiable value. The sections of the Customs Act which establish the method of determining value for duty were largely rewritten by Parliament in the summer of 1958, and it is the provisions in effect since that time which are discussed here.

CARDINAL PRINCIPLE OF VALUATION. Where the same goods as those imported into Canada are sold in the country of origin under competitive conditions in the same quantities, the value for duty is the price at which those goods are sold—that is, their "fair market value". This is the cardinal principle of valuation and is used for about three-quarters of the importations into Canada.

In applying this "like goods" rule, as set down in Section 36 of the Customs Act, certain legislative provisions are followed. For instance, if there are no sales at the time the goods are shipped to Canada, the most recent sales are taken. If there are no purchasers located at the place of origin, sales to the nearest purchasers are substituted. Where there are no purchasers in the export country at the same wholesale or retail trade level as the Canadian importer, the purchasers at the trade level subsequent to that of the importer are substituted, this procedure usually being followed for importations by Canadian national distributors who generally have no counterpart in the United States. Finally, the Department of National Revenue does not necessarily recognize sales to wholly-owned subsidiaries or controlled companies as "arms-length" transactions; in other words, these may not be free transactions under competitive conditions and may not necessarily represent fair market value.

SIMILAR GOODS RULE. If the fair market value of like goods cannot be determined due to the absence of relevant transactions, then the "similar goods" rule is employed. The "similar goods" rule is found under Section 37 of the Customs Act, and states that the value for duty is the cost of production of the imported goods plus the same gross profit mark-up as that on similar goods sold in the country of origin. For example, if certain beans are brought into Canada from the United States in 12-ounce packages and are sold only in 10-ounce packages in the United States home market, the dutiable value is the production cost of the beans in 12-ounce packages plus the same mark-up (say 35 percent) as that on the 10-ounce packages. Obviously, the application of a similar goods rule, without an allowance for the difference in production costs between the goods imported and the similar goods used for comparison, would be extremely limited.

In the great majority of cases, the value can be determined under the like goods or similar goods rule with some degree of certainty; and accordingly the fair market valuation method is employed. In fact, it is safe to say that these two rules are followed in valuing nearly all normal trade.

MINISTERIAL RULE. Where appropriate transactions do not occur in the country of export to allow the like goods or similar goods rule to be applied, the value is determined in such manner as the Minister of National Revenue prescribes, in accordance with Section 38 of the Customs Act. The type of transactions valued in this manner are imports originating in countries where competitive conditions do not exist in the home market (for example, in cases in which a state trading monopoly exists), the importation of architectural plans and the importation of correspondence courses where the total price to the Canadian importer reflects both the cost of the books used and a tuition fee.

In addition, Section 38 enumerates a number of specific situations where the ministerial rule shall apply. One situation is where the imported goods are intended to be assembled, packaged, or further manufactured in Canada, or are intended to enter into the course of manufacture in Canada. The reasoning here is that the application of the like or similar goods rule might detrimentally affect a Canadian producer. For example, if goods entering Canada to be packaged in Canada were given a valuation which made no allowance for the cost of packaging in Canada, the valuation would be higher than it should be and the result would be that the packaging would be done in the country of origin.

In the case of imports intended for further processing in Canada, such as semi-finished pharmaceuticals, the like or similar goods rule application might discourage work being done in Canada at all. On the other hand, certain of the situations enumerated represent an effort to discourage special types of importations which may undercut domestic competition, such as used or obsolete goods, job lots, remnants, close-outs, discontinued lines, and surplus goods.

COST-OF-PRODUCTION METHOD. Where the Minister of National Revenue is satisfied that a Canadian industry is being injured materially by the importation of goods whose value for duty under the ordinary methods, as outlined above, is less than their cost of production plus a reasonable gross profit (that is, the mark-up ordinarily taken in the particular industry concerned), then the Cabinet may increase the value for duty by an amount equal to the difference. An order in council under this section (Section 39) cannot remain in force for more than one year and may be revoked sooner. Its purpose is to provide one means for dealing with goods that are dumped into Canada.

PRICE-AVERAGING PROVISION. The Customs Act provides that the Minister of National Revenue, in cases where he considers that the market price at the time of shipment is abnormally low, may value manufactured goods and fresh fruits and vegetables of a class or kind produced in Canada at an average of the market prices prevailing in the export country over a certain period prior to shipment. For manufactured goods, the averaging period is any reasonable period, having regard to the particular industry concerned; for fresh fruits and vegetables (for example, frozen peas), the period is three years prior to shipment.

DUMPING DUTIES. Under the Customs Tariff Act, if goods of a class or kind made or produced in Canada are sold to a Canadian importer at a lower price than the value for duty, as determined under provisions outlined above, then a special dumping duty is levied on them equal to the difference. The dumping duty cannot exceed fifty percent ad valorem and the Cabinet may exempt any particular class of goods. Remnants, job lots, used and second-hand goods, once exempt from anti-dumping duties, are now subject to them. In January 1959, deductions in a range of 5 percent to 10 percent from the price of certain textiles were specified as the maximum permissible when these goods are entered as "seconds". It is estimated that almost 75 percent of recent imports of cotton fabrics from the United States have been alleged "seconds".[1]

When the "price-averaging" method of determining dutiable value is employed, the effect is to prevent the entry of goods at temporarily or seasonally low prices, even though the same low price prevails in the home market. Of particular concern here are end-of-season or end-of-line goods purchased from the United States at bargain prices. For instance, the peak production and marketing period for many fresh fruits and vegetables growing in the United States precedes that in Canada and, without restriction, end-of-season products at low prices would come into the Canadian market just at its seasonal peak when domestic producers expect to obtain their best prices. Similarly, style goods, such as clothing, tend to have an earlier seasonal peak in the United States than in Canada, and the price-averaging valuation method is often utilized.

The purpose of the cost-of-production valuation method is to restrict the entry of goods into Canada at distress prices, even though these same prices prevail in the home market and there is no question of an advanced seasonal or marketing period. There has thus far been no application of this valuation method.

What in fact constitutes "dumping" and should be prevented, is a difficult matter and will not be discussed at any length here. The opinion might be ventured, however, that it is *temporary* cheapness of imports which justifies the application of dumping duties.

If conditions are such that the dumping can be expected to continue more or less permanently, there would be no economic case for interference. Cheapness, as long as it is permanent cheapness, provides an economic gain rather than a loss to the economy receiving the dumped goods. If, however, the dumping tends to be sporadic, as has normally been the

1. *The Financial Post*, Toronto, January 31, 1959.

case in Canada, then it can be argued that the disruptive effect on domestic industries may more than offset any temporary gain to consumers.[1]

It is true that this sporadic type of dumping has been especially troublesome for Canada, and quite often the source of the dumped goods has been the United States. From time to time, certain U.S. firms have found it advantageous to ship goods in excess of domestic requirements to Canada at a price slightly above their prime costs but lower than the U.S. market price. The entry of these goods into the relatively small Canadian market has sometimes had a very disturbing effect, and it is this kind of dumping which Canadian customs legislation is primarily designed to prevent.

Due to their hidden, discriminating nature, the anti-dumping provisions have a potential for mischievous abuse. It should be noted that Canadian legislation does not require proof of injury to domestic producers before arbitrary valuations can be applied and dumping duties assessed. However, one can venture the opinion that during the postwar period, Canada has not made extensive use of the valuation process as a deliberate means of restricting trade, and that, for all practical purposes, the valuation process probably has not been significant in determining the level of protection. On the other hand, this assertion is difficult to prove, since no one has yet found a meaningful method of measuring its restrictiveness. One can calculate the amount of dumping duties collected over a period, and the number of times arbitrary valuation procedures were used, but, as in the case of ordinary tariffs, this provides no indication of how many items were prevented from entering because importers anticipated the application of restrictive duties.

Liquidation and Litigation

LIQUIDATION

The amount of duty originally paid on entering a commodity may be changed later by the Customs administration. In some cases, the importer may receive a refund of duty paid or, on the other hand, he may be required to pay additional duties. Under the Customs Act, the chief appraiser's office in Ottawa reviews all entries at all ports, a copy of the entry documents being forwarded to him for this purpose. If he believes the original entry to be incorrect, he instructs the local official to secure an amended entry, and the difference in the amount of duty is settled. The entry is thereby finalized or liquidated. This system of central checking has the advantage of ensuring uniform treatment by all local port officials across the country.

The number of amended entries is relatively small. In 1951, for example, there were only 120,405 (4.4 percent of total import entries), and 21,040 of these involved refunds to importers. A great many others represented minor

---

1. Young, J. H., *Canadian Commercial Policy*, Royal Commission on Canada's Economic Prospects, November 1957, page 136.

corrections, the errors frequently being discovered by the local port officials themselves and corrected within a day or two. Amended entries do occur, however, up to a month or so after the original entry and, where the revision is upward, the importer receives an unpleasant surprise in many cases. In addition, there is no legal time limit on an amended entry requiring the payment of additional duties, and importers of commodities which are difficult to classify or value complain, since this adds to their uncertainties.

LITIGATION

The system of appeal from customs officials' decisions is a fairly simple one. Initial appeal is made from the local official's decision to the chief appraiser in Ottawa, and from him to the Deputy Minister of National Revenue (Customs Division), all in an informal manner and frequently by a telephone call or wire to Ottawa. In this way, most appeals are settled quickly by administrative action. There are, however, a limited number of appeals which go beyond the Deputy Minister to the Tariff Board. From April 1, 1949 to June 24, 1953, for instance, there were 136 such appeals, of which 24 were withdrawn and two were ruled outside the Board's jurisdiction. Finally, a decision of the Board may be appealed to the Exchequer Court on questions of law only, and from there to the Supreme Court of Canada, but such appeals have been rare.

Any decision of the Deputy Minister concerning tariff classification, value-for-duty, or eligibility for drawbacks, can be appealed to the Tariff Board by "any person who deems himself aggrieved" by such a decision, whether he is the importer or a domestic competitor. However, in order to compel a formal decision of the Deputy Minister which can be appealed to the Tariff Board, a domestic competitor must become an importer himself. To outline the procedure more fully, if a domestic competitor disagrees with a ruling of the customs officials, he may first of all register his disagreement with the Department of National Revenue. Then, if he is not satisfied with the explanation given him, he must import the article in question himself and appeal the entry to the Deputy Minister, thereby forcing a decision by the Deputy Minister from which an appeal can be made to the Board on the grounds that the domestic competitor as an importer has been treated too leniently.

The relatively small number of appeals to the Tariff Board in part reflects the considerable discretionary authority given to the Customs administration. That is, the Deputy Minister has the power to make various departmental regulations for carrying out the provisions of the statutes, and grounds for appeal from his decisions are usually difficult to find. In addition, it reflects the attitude of importers that normally an appeal is not worth the time and expense involved, despite the fact that the Board's procedures are comparatively informal and its decisions brought down quite promptly—usually within a month or two. "It is likely, then, that cases coming before the

Tariff Board are special cases, in the sense that they are considered particularly vexatious by importers or contain *possibilities* of high monetary reward if successfully prevented."[1]

Since 1949, the Board has allowed about half of the appeals made to it. Most appeals have been on matters of classification, and few have concerned valuation. There were only two appeals by domestic competitors for higher valuations, and both were dismissed. The Board has held that when serious uncertainty concerning the interpretation of a tariff item exists, the ruling should be in favor of the importer. Where the importer has gone to great lengths to determine what duty is payable and the Board has ruled in favor of the higher amount charged, it has sometimes recommended to the Government that a refund be made.

Although the Board has frequently declared that the Department incorrectly classified goods and has specified that a different classification is applicable—in some cases, a different classification from that pleaded by the importer—it has been reluctant to differ with the Department on matters of valuation. To illustrate, in a 1952 appeal concerning the valuation of church blueprints, the Board stated:

> The method or practices followed by the Department in valuing blueprints and plans may not be necessarily the right one, as certainly it is not the only one that might be adopted. Nevertheless, the appellant in evidence failed to indicate what, in its stead, would be a just and proper method and, more precisely, a just and proper value.[2]

There are a large number of Canadian laws and regulations, apart from those dealing with the tariff and its administration, which create barriers of one kind or another to goods entering Canada from the United States. We have already discussed import controls in Chapter 3. Now let us examine some of the other more important non-tariff barriers.

Marking Requirements

Canada does not require that all imports be marked to show the country of origin. Instead, the Government may, by order in council, require specific types of goods to be marked, stamped, branded, or labeled in legible English or French words, in a conspicuous place that is not covered or obscured in any way, so as to indicate the country of origin; and the marking must be as nearly indelible and permanent as the nature of the goods will permit. At the present time, the order covers all printed material, certain paper bags and boxes, shoes, chinaware and porcelainware, household utensils and

---

1. Blake, Gordon, *Customs Administration in Canada*, University of Toronto Press, 1957, page 124.
2. Report of Tariff Board in Ref. No. 111, Engineers' and Architects' Plans, Ottawa, 1952.

ornaments, clocks, hats, shapes of felt, ribbons made of textile fibers, candles, and a few other items. If these goods do not conform to the marking regulations, they must be marked, before being released from customs, at the expense of the importer.

Although marking is only required for a limited number of commodities, to the foreign manufacturers and importers concerned it is just one more expense in moving goods across the border. To illustrate, in 1955, cotton sheets and pillow slips (which enter Canada chiefly from the United States) were added to the marking order. At that time, one competent and experienced importer estimated that the cost of meeting the new requirement could amount to as much as the equivalent of a 3 percent increase in the customs duty (which is 22½ percent). Chinaware and porcelainware must be marked during the manufacturing process before the pieces are fired in the kiln. A U.S. manufacturer of chinaware who might otherwise ship to Canada from time to time as the opportunity arises is prevented from doing so because his wares are not properly marked.

The marking order prescribes in some detail the content of the classes and the manner in which some of the goods are to be marked.[1] In addition, departmental regulations stipulate the method of marking certain other items. Occasionally disputes and delays occur over the method of marking to be used. For instance, the importer of a shipment of small perforated price tickets in booklets containing 100 each was initially told by the port officials that each individual ticket had to be stamped with the country of origin; eventually, however, the officials settled for each booklet being stamped. Another example is a shipment of fountain pens from the United States which was held at the border because the packages were marked rather than the pieces themselves; but an appeal to higher customs officials brought about the shipment's release.

Health, Sanitary and Quarantine Regulations

Canada maintains high standards as regards the importation and distribution of goods and drugs in order both to protect the consumer and to control animal and plant diseases. At the Federal level, there is the Food and Drugs Act, the Fruit, Vegetables and Honey Act, the Maple Products Industry Act, the Meat and Canned Foods Act, the Animals Contagious Act, the Destructive Insect and Pest Act, the Fish Inspection Act and several other statutes which provide for the inspection, grading, labeling and packaging of foods and drugs. These are supplemented by various provincial and

---

1. "This listing established by Order-in-Council can either expand or contract as far as the quantity of goods so affected is concerned. As the law is presently worded, this section of the Customs Tariff Act can be applied against goods where the demand for tariff protection from Canadian industry is the greatest". (Corbett, Murrary E., Legal Counsel, Canadian Importers and Traders Association, March 1958.)

municipal controls. Customs officials cooperate with and assist agriculture, food and drug authorities in the enforcement of these regulations.

Although the regulations apply to domestic trade as well as importations, they undoubtedly have more restrictive effects upon the latter. The reason is that in transborder trade, each shipment must come under the scrutiny of a customs examiner and other government inspectors, with the result that a higher proportion of shipments are actually inspected and analyzed than in the case of domestic shipments. An additional factor is the likelihood that information concerning regulations and any changes in them will be distributed more promptly and thoroughly to domestic producers than to foreign producers or importers. Although U.S. regulations do not differ from Canadian regulations to the extent that those of many other countries do, such differences as do exist undoubtedly cause importers of foodstuffs to exercise great care and restraint when contemplating the importation of a shipment, and thereby afford protection to domestic products.

An interesting feature of health and sanitary regulations is the difficulty faced by importers and foreign producers in attempting to obtain relief from their restrictive effects, even though their case might be quite sound. Take the case of a U.S. producer who objects to the treatment he has received from a Canadian health inspector. If he objects publicly, perhaps forcing an investigation, the result may be that doubt is cast upon the quality of his product in the minds of Canadian consumers and, regardless of the outcome of his argument with government officials or the merits of his case, his market may be damaged. For this reason, one hears few public complaints concerning the administration of Canada's, or any other country's, health and sanitation regulations.

Although it is impossible to discuss here all the many regulations controlling the traffic in food, animal and plant products, it might be worthwhile to mention a few of them for illustrative purposes. Shipments of meat and meat products, for example, are refused entry at the border unless the standard of meat inspection in the exporting country is ruled satisfactory and an approved certificate of inspection is submitted. These requirements appear to present no serious obstacles in the United States. However, until recently pork had to be cooked before it could be imported into Canada, despite the fact that raw U.S. pork was being exported to the U.K. upon certification as originating in states not allowing vaccination with live cholera virus, and other importers of U.S. pork, such as Germany, Holland, France, Belgium, Denmark and Sweden, required no certification regarding freedom from animal disease.[1]

---

1. The U.S. federal quarantine for vesicular exanthema, a serious disease of swine, was lifted from two townships in one county of New Jersey in October 1959. The removal of these U.S. regulations completely eliminated the medical justification for this Canadian embargo, since there had not been a case of this disease in the United States for three years. The Canadian embargo was lifted in February 1960.

Shipments of preserved fruits and vegetables must be accompanied by an affidavit from the shipper that the product was processed under the prescribed sanitary conditions; that it is sound, wholesome and fit for human food; that the containers show the name and address of the manufacturer or fruit dealer; and that the description of the contents is true and conforms to quality, container, and labeling requirements. Agents, dealers, or brokers engaging in interprovincial or international trade in fresh fruits and vegetables must be licensed; and each importation must be accompanied by a government inspection certificate of the country of origin stating that it meets Canadian regulations and the containers must be marked "Inspected for Export".

Certain trade is affected by special Federal specifications over and above quality and sanitary standards. Thus, fresh fruits and canned goods may be sold only in containers of specified sizes, not always identical with U.S. domestic market practice. U.S. peaches, for example, can be sold only in one-half bushel or bushel baskets, although a ruling in July 1959 finally permitted their importation in wirebound crates to prevent damage in transit. Provincial regulations and Federal home loan regulations require electrical apparatus to pass Canadian quality standards certification, which entails the payment of substantial fees and the opening of manufacturing processes to inspection.

Although the Food and Drugs Act requires inspectors to pay for samples obtained in domestic trade, the same is not true for imported goods. Thus, an importer loses that part of each shipment which is taken as a sample in cases where inspection or analysis renders the sample unmarketable. Some importers suspect that occasionally samples are taken which are larger than technically required or which may even be unauthorized. "Moreover, when one or more cases of a tempting or valuable delicacy are opened and left in the customs warehouses, the passerby is sorely tempted to do his own testing. The disappearances may form a relatively small proportion of a large shipment, but, as one importer remarked, 'Ten percent of a $40,000 shipment of candy isn't peanuts'."[1]

Other features of the health and quarantine legislation also bear critical examination. One example is a regulation under the Fruit, Vegetables and Honey Act which prohibits the entry of fresh fruits and vegetables unless "accompanied by conclusive evidence that the importer purchased such goods not later than 24 hours after the time of shipment from the point of production." The only apparent reason for such a provision is to prevent the importation of produce shipped at the height of the marketing season in the United States without being first sold and allowed to move, or "roll", from one area to another until reaching a market where prices are not too

---

1. Elliott, G. A., *op. cit.*, page 249.

low. Prior to this regulation, these "rollers" from the United States frequently found their way on to the Canadian market where they would be sold at prices lower than they could be marketed through regular channels.

Protection of Industrial Property Rights

Canada, like the United States and most other countries, has laws preventing the importation of articles which would, if sold in Canada, infringe upon certain industrial property rights—namely, patents, copyrights and trade-marks. With respect to trade-marks, Schedule C of the Customs Tariff Act prohibits the importation of articles which have been prohibited by a Court order under the Trade-Marks Act due to a breach of that statute. In the case of copyrights, Schedule C prohibits the importation of unauthorized reprints of Canadian copyrighted works. The definition of what constitutes an unauthorized reprint, however, and the manner by which its presence is made known to customs officials, is found in Section 27 of the Copyright Act. It states:

> Copies made out of Canada of any work in which copyright subsists that if made in Canada would infringe copyright and as to which the owner of the copyright gives notice in writing to the Department of National Revenue that he is desirous that such copies should not be so imported into Canada, shall not be so imported, and shall be deemed to be included in Schedule C of the Customs Tariff, and that Schedule shall apply accordingly.

The onus, therefore, is on an injured patentee to see that the import in question is prohibited from entry rather than on the Customs administration.

In connection with copyrights, the recent Royal Commission on Patents, Copyrights, Trade-marks and Industrial Designs, in its Report on Copyrights (1957), reveals an interesting attempt by Canadian book companies to have certain book imports prohibited. Most of the books handled by these companies are imported from publishers in the United States, the United Kingdom and France, and distributed by them as exclusive agents. For the most part, the Canadian copyrights are held by the foreign publishers. From time to time, a company would attempt to employ Section 27 of the Act to prohibit the importation by any other firm of a certain book published by the Canadian copyright holder abroad, and for which they held the exclusive distribution rights in Canada. The Commission obtained a legal opinion from the Department of Justice, which said that such prohibitions could not be supported by the existing legislation. The opinion added that if such books were placed in Schedule C, they would be barred from importation by anyone, including the exclusive agent. The Royal Commission did not recommend that the legislation be amended in order to forbid such imports, despite concerted efforts on the part of the Canadian book companies to have it do so.

The Canadian Patent Act provides for the granting of exclusive rights to successful applicants not only to manufacture the patented article but also to import it into Canada. The Act goes even further, however, and in Section 67 says that the exclusive rights under a Canadian patent shall be deemed to be abused if the manufacture of the invention within Canada on a commercial scale is being prevented or hindered by the importation of the patented article into Canada. Patents for new inventions, the Act holds, "are granted not only to encourage invention but to secure the new inventions shall so far as possible be worked on a commercial scale in Canada without undue delay."

If the Commissioner of Patents is satisfied that a case of abuse has been established, he may grant a compulsory license to any party willing and able to manufacture the patented article in Canada, and if this does not remedy the fault, he may revoke the patent. Obviously, the result of these provisions is largely to eliminate the importation of patented articles wherever it is feasible for them to be produced commercially in Canada.

The reasoning behind Section 67 is not difficult to understand. By far the greatest proportion of North American inventions occur in the United States, and were it not for these provisions, American businessmen could refuse to license their Canadian patents to Canadian manufacturers, thereby preventing the production of the patented articles in Canada. Tariffs could not afford the kind of protection given domestic manufacturers by Section 67. The total number of patents issued in Canada during the last five government fiscal years, together with the number of inventors resident in Canada and the United States are listed in Table 11.

TABLE 11

Patents Issued in Canada,
and Number of Inventors Resident in Canada and the United States,
1953-1958

Fiscal Year	Total Patents Issued	Inventors Resident in Canada	Inventors Resident in U.S.
1953-54	9,405	603 (6%)	6,849 (73%)
1954-55	10,274	570 (6%)	7,719 (75%)
1955-56	11,840	652 (6%)	8,583 (72%)
1956-57	15,494	761 (5%)	11,131 (72%)
1957-58	16,248	772 (5%)	11,695 (74%)

Source: McConnell, B., "Memorandum regarding the imposition of United States laws upon Canadian firms operating in Canada" (unpublished).

Perhaps the most publicized example of the restrictive effect of Section 67 on imports from the United States concerns radio and television sets. There is in Canada a patent pooling company called Canadian Radio Patents Limited, which owns thousands of patents relating to radio and television sets. Since this company will only license their patents to domestic manufacturers and not to importers, importations into Canada of radio and television sets for resale are in effect prohibited. This prohibition, however, has recently been lifted in the case of patents held by one large U.S. subsidiary in Canada. In October 1958, the RCA Victor Company Limited complied with a consent order of the U.S. Government, the purpose of which was to make available all the company's Canadian patents to the U.S. parent corporation and to give the parent company the right to export to Canada. The Canadian subsidiary was required to withdraw from the patent pool.

Government Procurement Policies

Like most other governments, the Canadian Government favours the domestic producer when it comes to spending the taxpayers' money, and, by so doing, establishes indirect trade barriers against the importation of a wide variety of foreign goods. There is not, however, any legislation or written body of rules which sets down or governs the nature or extent of this discrimination. It is simply a matter of public policy to favour Canadian industry, and this policy may vary from one type of expenditure to another, and from one year to the next. For this reason, it is impossible to pin down in any exact manner the degree of preference given Canadian firms over U.S. firms or to begin to measure the restrictive effects on imports from the United States. Nevertheless, certain general comments can be made.

In the area of defense spending, which is by far the largest single class of public expenditure at the federal level, it can safely be said that Canada buys a much larger proportion of her requirements abroad than do many other technologically advanced countries, including the United States and Great Britain. Furthermore, most of the foreign buying is from the United States. This situation is not particularly the result of a liberal government policy, but is largely due to inescapable economic and business considerations. That is to say, Canada cannot manufacture certain defense items—especially the larger, more complex ones—as efficiently as the United States because of the smaller market and limited production runs. Therefore, one finds that a considerable amount of Canadian defense spending takes place in the United States either directly, through primary contracts or, more important, indirectly, through sub-contracts.

In 1958, the value of expenditures on defense contracts placed directly in the United States amounted to $41.7 million (compared to $13.2 million in the United Kingdom). With respect to sub-contracts, it is estimated that in the neighbourhood of $75 million of such expenditures were made in the United States in the same year. This means that during 1958, U.S. producers obtained about 15 percent of total Canadian defense-contract expenditures. The bulk of the spending was on aircraft and electronic and communication equipment.

Policy with respect to government procurement is naturally based on many factors—some economic, some strategic and some political. Generally speaking, it would be correct to say that goods are purchased from domestic sources if produced on a reasonably economic basis and if the preference margin is not "unreasonably" wide, although no indication is available as to what constitutes an "unreasonable" margin. One finds that many standard items, such as clothing and equipage, fuels and lubricants, small arms and ammunition and construction materials are almost exclusively acquired from Canadian companies.

In addition, where Canadian industry is equipped and anxious to manufacture large, expensive items, as in the case of destroyers, the contracts are always placed in the home market. In the case of aircraft, missiles, and electronic apparatus, where extensive research and developmental programming are required, procurement is a matter of high-level policy, and, as the recent cancellation of the Avro Arrow manned jet interceptor contract indicates, is constantly under review and subject to reappraisal. Certainly, regarding expenditures on these broad defense programs, Canada will never be self-sufficient, and will continue to spend a large portion of its defense dollar in the United States.

Although public expenditure in non-defense areas is similarly biased in favor of domestic producers, the margin of preference is lower due to the absence of strategic considerations. A buy-Canadian bias exists in the purchases of all government departments, and, in many instances, foreign firms are not even asked to tender on contracts. However, it is not easy to document specific cases where results would appear to be unwarranted. In provinces which have established government liquor stores, few U.S. products are stocked, allegedly because of the small demand for them. Local and Commonwealth producers of beer and wine are particularly favoured by these government establishments. Where foreign spirits are made available, protection is given the domestic product by applying a much higher mark-up to the foreign spirits.

Conclusions

Canadian administrative or indirect trade barriers undoubtedly impose a burden on many U.S. firms exporting to Canada, just as similar U.S. barriers impose a burden on many Canadian firms exporting to the United States. At the same time, however, there is no reason to believe that this burden is heavier for U.S. exporters than for those of other foreign countries, nor that it is particularly severe when considered in the light of world trading practices as a whole. Nevertheless, these "invisible" barriers are multitudinous, and make their effects felt in a variety of ways. An American who has not had previous experience in exporting dog biscuits to Canada may find, to his surprise, that the value for duty is considerably higher than he had anticipated because, although he is selling in bulk to a Canadian distributor, the valuation is based on the retail sales his firm makes in the home market. A U.S. canning company may suddenly learn that a shipment of canned tomatoes has been stopped at the border because of an improper label. An importer bringing air rifles in from the United States may be informed, to his dismay, that the rifles are of a class or kind made in Canada, and are therefore subject to a higher rate of duty than he had counted on.

These administrative barriers, in one way or another, mean higher costs for U.S. companies selling to the Canadian market. All exporters, even established ones making routine shipments, must employ people to handle the paper work required in moving their goods across the border and, in addition, they must continually watch for any changes in Canadian legislation, regulations or practices which might possibly have a bearing on their operations.

The most restrictive effects, however, appear to be on U.S. companies entering the Canadian market for the first time, or on firms marketing new products in Canada. For it is in these areas of trade that the problem of uncertainty is most keenly felt. A U.S. firm looking toward the Canadian market for the first time may hesitate to engage in this trade because of the special efforts required to learn the mechanics of moving goods across the border and a fear of how goods will be treated by customs officials. Similarly, a company which has created a new product may think twice before exporting it to Canada, believing that it may be difficult to determine the duty payable. Unfortunately, the curtailment of new trade channels is one of the most serious penalties Canada must accept for maintaining a complex customs system.

Gordon Blake comments on the uncertainties, delays and costs under discussion here:

"The importing community is primarily concerned with its laid-down costs and with the disposing of its goods in a reasonably short time at mark-ups which, in the state of modern competition, may be rather closely calculated . . . An importer who is plagued by uncertainty as to what his laid-down costs ultimately will be will react in one of two ways. If sufficiently worried he will reduce or discontinue the importation of the troublesome commodities. Staple, low-cost items with a moderate mark-up appear to be particularly affected in this way. On the other hand, he may accept the fact of uncertainty as an element in his costs, and he will then be induced to increase his mark-up in an attempt to ensure himself against the likelihood of unpleasant surprises and financial losses in the unstable area of his customs activities. In either case, the burden of this protection in excess of that implied by the tariff rate 'per se' tends to be shifted forward to the consumer, or backward to the exporter. Uncertainty is being translated into economic cost."[1]

---

1. Gordon Blake, *Customs Administration in Canada*, University of Toronto Press, 1957, p. 134.

6

Effects of
U.S. Trade Barriers

THIS CHAPTER designates some Canadian industries which are affected by U.S. trade restrictions. Except in a general qualitative fashion, it does not attempt to assess the degree to which they are excluded from the U.S. market. A much more intensive study of specific industries would be required to indicate the extent to which Canadian industries would benefit from a lowering of the U.S. tariff. Available statistical information on trade reflects numerous and varied influences, and no ready technique has yet been devised which would enable an easy identification of the effects or an accurate weighting of their relative importance. Trade restrictions do not exist in isolation; foreign trade is influenced by political and social changes, business fluctuations, technological developments, shifts in consumers' tastes and spending patterns, market structures, and types of business organization.

Tariff schedules alone, even when diligently dissected, tell only part of the story of barriers to trade. In a growing economy, owing to changes in relative costs, the degree of protection of any given restriction undergoes constant alteration. Conclusions arrived at one time may have no significance at a later date—for example, the fact that a tariff exists does not always mean that it restricts trade. Moreover, restrictions of certain imports may, by eliminating competitors for the consumer's dollar, increase the demand for other foreign products. Hence, the over-all effect of import restrictions will differ from that of a given tariff or quota by itself.

Some Canadian commodities which may be affected by U.S. trade barriers are examined in this section under three broad categories—agricultural and fish products; industrial raw materials and fuels; and manufactured goods. It should be emphasized that this is not a comprehensive listing, and that the observations which follow are tentative, and subject to change as a result of altered market conditions.

Agricultural Commodities and Fish Products

The agricultural and fishing industries of Canada, and the industries based on them, are affected unevenly by U.S. trade restrictions (see Table 12). Wheat is by far the most important single commodity facing restricted entry to the United States. Wheat prices in Canada are significantly lower than the landed price in the United States, duty included. An absolute quota of only 800,000 bushels, imposed under Section 22 of the Agriculture Adjustment Act, prevents any significant quantity of exports to the United States. Seed wheat and wheat unfit for human consumption are both excluded from the quota, and wheat unfit for human consumption is subject to a duty less than half as high. Hence the problem of classification has attracted considerable attention. Legislation to prevent the importation of seed wheat declared "unfit for human consumption" when treated with a poisonous fungicide was vetoed by the President in 1958. It is difficult to see how the United States can maintain a normal market for wheat as long as the price-support program keeps U.S. prices roughly a third higher than those in Canada for comparable grades.[1]

TABLE 12

U.S. Trade Restrictions on Selected Canadian Agricultural Commodities and Fish Products

Item	Estimated Ad Valorem Equivalent of Tariff (November 1958)	Quota	Probable Current Effect of Trade Restrictions
Whole milk.................	5	absolute	slight
Apparel wool...............	22	none	insignificant
Live cattle.................	5 to 9	tariff	insignificant
Beef and veal...............	7	none	insignificant
Beef and veal, prepared or preserved.................	10	none	slight
Pork, prepared or preserved...	4 to 6	none	slight
Butter.....................	12	absolute	insignificant
Cheddar cheese.............	15	absolute	slight
Fish, fresh or frozen..........	4 to 8	tariff if filleted or frozen blocks	slight
Barley.....................	4	none	insignificant
Oats.......................	6	none	insignificant
Rye.......................	5	absolute	substantial
Wheat, for human consumption...............	11	absolute	substantial
Clover seed.................	0.1 to 1.0	none	slight
Alfalfa seed.................	4	none	slight
Potatoes...................	18 to 36	tariff	substantial
Bovine hides and skins........	4[1]	none	insignificant
Bovine leather..............	8½ to 12½[1]	none	slight
Flaxseed and linseed oil.......	67 to 85	none	very substantial

1. Ad valorem rate.

1. The study entitled "Wheat Surpluses and Their Impact on Canada-United States Relations", by W. E. Hamilton and W. M. Drummond (Canadian-American Committee, sponsored by the National Planning Association and Private Planning Association of Canada, 1959), outlines the Canadian and U.S. policies affecting wheat production and marketing, and analyzes the surplus problems in considerable detail.

Imports of wheat milling products (wheat flour, semolina, crushed or cracked wheat, and similar products) are also restricted, more by an absolute quota of four million pounds than by the relatively low duty of 52 cents per hundred pounds. Canada is assigned the lion's share of the quota—3,815,000 pounds. The restrictions on milling products are insignificant in relation to the over-all picture. Wheat is more easily shipped to milling facilities, and trade in flour would not be important in the absence of restrictions on wheat imports. Cake and confectionery mixes are exempt from this quota.

The duties on barley, oats and rye have always been low. The U.S. import-export picture fluctuates from year to year, depending on growing conditions, the returns from alternate uses of land (especially wheat), and developments in government price-support programs. An absolute quota on U.S. imports of rye limits the total to 186 million pounds annually, or roughly one-fifth of U.S. production. Of this, 182,280,000 pounds are assigned to Canada. Although before World War II, the United States was normally a net exporter of rye, high support prices for wheat have caused domestic production to fall below consumption. As recently as 1951, U.S. imports equalled only one-twelfth of domestic production. However, for several years the Canadian quota for rye has been filled, indicating that the quota appears to be a substantial obstacle to imports. Oats, on the other hand, would probably have moved, net, from the United States into Canada during the 1958-59 crop year in the absence of trade barriers.

While it is true that a very high tariff is levied on apparel wool, a number of factors would suggest that it may not be very restrictive as regards Canadian-produced wool. For example, Australia, New Zealand, Argentina and other countries would seem to have competitive advantages in climate and supplies of cheap land and labor.

In the case of cattle, beef, veal and pork, U.S. imports, and especially imports from Canada, fluctuate widely in response to varying price relationships as regards foreign markets. It is likely that some Canadian, Australian and New Zealand meat will continue to enter the United States. Tariffs vary from five to ten percent, and there are no quotas or restrictive sanitary restrictions on the U.S. side. Canadian products should be able to surmount the existing barriers with little difficulty.

The U.S. market for bacon, hams and shoulders is significant. Although some 19 countries exported these products to the United States in 1957, more than 90 percent of total U.S. imports of hams and shoulders was accounted for by the Netherlands, Poland, Denmark and Western Germany. The same factors which make it unlikely that U.S. trade barriers on cattle, beef and veal are particularly restrictive to Canadian producers also apply with respect to the bulk of Canadian prepared or preserved pork products.

The degree to which U.S. trade barriers inhibit the transborder movement of fresh milk is uncertain. Authority exists under the Agricultural Adjustment Act to impose additional fees or quotas on the importation of commodities if such importation tends to render ineffective or materially interfere with any price-support or other program relating to agricultural commodities. Although price-supports are in effect on milk, this authority has never been used. Import curbs currently in effect do include a tariff of two cents per gallon and a quota of three million gallons per year, imposed by the Tariff Act of 1930. However, virtually no fresh milk enters the United States. This may, however, be largely due to sanitary restrictions imposed by state and municipal authorities, and perhaps, to a lesser extent to insufficient price incentives to cause Canadian farmers to seek U.S. markets. U.S. prices of Class-1 milk—for consumption as fresh milk—are somewhat lower than Canadian prices in the West (e.g., Vancouver-Seattle) and somewhat higher in the East (e.g., New York-Montreal). Allowing for freight, the "net-back" to farmers in Quebec and Ontario who may consider shipping to New York would appear to be about the same as derived from shipping to Montreal. The knowledge that penetration of the U.S. market in volume might result in higher U.S. barriers is perhaps also an important factor in preventing transborder trade in fresh milk.

By world standards, both Canada and the United States are relatively high-cost producers of butter and cheese. The U.S. market for butter is protected by a miniscule import quota of 707,000 pounds, and only incidentally by the tariff of seven cents per pound. Imports in 1958 were distributed among the following countries: Canada, Brazil, Argentina, Sweden, Denmark, the U.K., Australia and New Zealand. Imports from Canada were insignificant. During the decade of the 'thirties, other countries—principally the Netherlands, the Soviet Union, and Latvia—supplied substantial amounts, and would undoubtedly offer powerful competition to Canada in case of reduction of U.S. import restrictions. Also, Canada now has a support price for butter of 64 cents per pound, which is higher than the U.S. support price of 55.75-58.75 cents. The U.S. quota would hardly appear to be restrictive to Canadian butter producers in this situation.

An absolute quota of less than one percent of domestic production is the major barrier to imports of cheddar (American) cheese into the United States. It is the type most commonly used in this country, and foreign production would appear to be highly competitive in the growing U.S. market. Cheddar cheese is produced for export in a great many countries, and would enter the United States in vastly increased quantities in the absence of tariffs and quotas. However, the effective Canadian support prices are 34.3-34.8 cents per pound, as compared with U.S. support prices of 32.75 cents. However, premium-price Canadian cheeses are now sold in quantity in the United Kingdom, and might also find substantial markets in the United States if free entry were permitted.

The tariffs on types of fish which compose the bulk of U.S. imports from Canada (cod, cusk, eels, haddock, hake, pollock, shad, sturgeon, fresh-water fish, halibut, salmon and mackerel, except frozen mackerel) are relatively low: one-half cent per pound whether or not whole, but not otherwise prepared or preserved; and 1.5 to 1.875 cents, if otherwise processed. It is doubtful whether these low duties affect trade to any extent. A tariff quota exists on groundfish "otherwise processed" (that is, fillets or frozen blocks). This amounts to either 15 million pounds or 15 percent of the average U.S. consumption of such fish during the preceding three calendar years, whichever is greater. Groundfish fillets entering in any quantity over the quota, are assessed at 2.5 cents, which is equivalent to about eight percent ad valorem equivalent. This may represent a modest barrier to imports.

During years of short crops, hardy varieties of clover and alfalfa seed are shipped from Canada in large quantities. In 1957, for example, red cloverseed imports were more than one-twentieth of the domestic production, while alfalfa seed imports were insignificant. In other years, the relation has been reversed. Domestic production normally covers virtually all of U.S. consumption. The relatively low tariff duty probably does not greatly affect the volume of imports.

Potatoes, both "table stock" and "seed potatoes", are subject to very high duties. For seed potatoes, certified by a responsible officer or agency of a foreign government, in accordance with official rules and regulations, to have been grown and approved especially for use as seed, 1,900,000 bushels may be imported each year, with a duty of 37½ cents per hundredweight. More restrictive is the tariff quota on potatoes for table use, which permits only 600,000 bushels to come in at the 37½-cent rate.[1]

The competitive advantage of the Canadian products is so great that despite these restrictions, imports have regularly been in excess of entries permitted at the reduced rate of duty. It would seem that they do keep out substantial amounts of both seed potatoes and table stock, at least in good potato years.

Bovine hides, skins and leather provide the classic example of a "joint product", with supply depending largely upon conditions in world markets for beef and veal. Much leather is not utilized due to high transportation and handling costs, and considerable excess capacity exists throughout the world. Some twenty countries export these products to the United States in competition with Canada, as certain imported leathers are highly competitive

1. However, if the production of white or Irish potatoes, including seed potatoes, according to the estimate of the U.S. Department of Agriculture made as of September 1, is less than 21 billion pounds, an additional quantity of potatoes equal to the amount by which such estimated production is less than 21 billion pounds shall be added to the 600,000 bushels provided for table stock. These quotas run from September 15 to September 15 of the following year.

with the domestic product. Reduction of the rates of duty on leather would doubtless greatly expand imports, as many producers have facilities for expanding production. Canada would certainly receive some benefit, although the price-elasticity of supply in that country is probably not high.[1]

On flaxseed and linseed oil, for fear that the high tariff (equivalent to 17 and 35 percent ad valorem) would not be sufficiently effective in limiting imports, a second line of defense, in the form of an additional fee of 50 percent ad valorem, has been added. These measures have succeeded in cutting imports to less than a trickle. Canadian producers have obviously been affected, and Canadian exports have been deflected to overseas countries.

Industrial Raw Materials and Fuels

Taken as a whole, U.S. tariffs on dutiable raw materials and fuels are relatively low, since these affect production costs of virtually all industrial firms. The tariffs range from 1 percent to 50 percent, ad valorem equivalent, but the majority are under 10 percent. Although the U.S. import barriers affect virtually all of the commodities listed in Table 13, they appear to be relatively unimportant in the case of finished petroleum products, nickel, acid-grade fluorspar, pig aluminum, lumber, and unmanufactured copper.

TABLE 13

U.S. Trade Restrictions on Selected Canadian Industrial Raw Materials and Fuels

Item	Estimated Ad Valorem Equivalent of Tariff (November 1958)	Quota	Probable Current Effect of Trade Restrictions
Crude barite....................	43	none	very substantial
Crude and unfinished oils.........	3 to 4	absolute[1]	insignificant
Residual fuel oil.................	5	absolute[1]	insignificant
Finished petroleum products.......	9 to 12	absolute[1]	slight
Lead-bearing ores...............	6	absolute	substantial
Refined lead....................	11	absolute	substantial
Zinc ore.......................	9	absolute	substantial
Refined zinc....................	8	absolute	substantial
Nickel.........................	2 to 17½[2]	none	insignificant
Fluorspar, metallurgical grade.....	34	none	substantial
Fluorspar, acid grade............	4	none	insignificant
Aluminum, pig..................	5	none	insignificant
Aluminum plates, sheets and bars..	8	none	substantial
Magnesium, pig.................	50[2]	none	substantial
Softwood lumber................	1	none	insignificant
Hardwood lumber...............	1 to 16⅔[2]	none	slight
Copper ores, concentrates and metal....................	6	none	slight
Copper in rolls, sheets and rods....	7	none	slight
Copper wire....................	17	none	substantial
Copper tubing..................	12	none	substantial

1. Imports from Canada are currently exempted.
2. Ad valorem rate.

1. See discussion of cattle, beef and veal above.

72

Barite is extracted from a very large deposit in Nova Scotia by open pit methods. The mine is favourably located for water transportation to Atlantic Coast ports, and is competitive with U.S. mines despite the very high tariff. In the absence of the U.S. tariff, large quantities of Canadian barite might well go to U.S. rather than to European markets.

The relatively low import-excise tax on crude oil may not affect trade, so long as foreign sources of supply continue to be complementary to the domestic ones. Gasoline is imported only in small quantities, as crude oil and residual fuel oils constitute the bulk of the imports. The tariff is significantly higher for gasoline than for crude oil, and it may have an impact in isolated areas of the United States which could be more easily served from Canadian refineries.

Domestic refiners are gradually increasing their yield of gasoline and distillate fuel oil at the expense of residual fuel oil. The latter product has increased in importance from one-fifth of total imports of petroleum and products in 1929 to approximately one-third today. This trend will probably continue regardless of the tariff, although the tax probably has had some effect upon the location of refining facilities, and thus may affect the composition of trade in the long run. Like gasoline, lubricating oils are not imported into the United States in large quantities for technical reasons, and the tariff is not an important restriction on trade.

During the postwar period, stockpile acquisitions of lead and zinc by the United States and the United Kingdom maintained world production far in excess of world industrial consumption. As a measure of the serious disturbance to the industry occasioned by a termination of stockpile acquisitions, the cut-back in world production necessary to achieve a balance in supply and demand for lead is estimated to be in excess of 125,000 tons, or five percent of world mine production.[1]

The relatively low tariff duties on lead and zinc ores and refined metal seem to have had little effect in restricting imports over the past 25 years. Many U.S. high-grade deposits have been depleted, and it is obvious that the United States has become and will remain dependent upon foreign sources for substantial quantities. Domestic mine production of lead is now only about one-half of the level attained in the late 1920's, while consumption by American industries has approximately doubled.

Smelting and refining operations enjoy a much greater degree of tariff protection than do mining and milling. The margin between the tariff duties on ores and on the refined product is in excess of the cost of converting the ore to refined metal. However, the major restriction on imports of primary

---

1. Statement by the Under Secretary of the Interior, Hatfield Chilson, before the Ways and Means Committee of the House of Representatives, August 1, 1957, on H.R. 8527 and other identical measures to amend the Internal Revenue Code of 1954, to impose import taxes on lead and zinc.

lead is an annual quota, equivalent to 80 percent of average imports during the five-year period 1953-57. The quota is allocated among exporting countries and subdivided by calendar quarters as to ores and concentrates and smelter products. Under this formula, the annual Canadian quotas are as follows:

ores and concentrates............ 6,720 short tons
smelter products[1]................ 7,960 short tons

Most of the observations made above in connection with import restrictions on lead are equally true of zinc. Import duties are not sufficiently high to exclude zinc from richer foreign deposits, and have not prevented a sharp decline in domestic production. Import quotas currently in effect for Canada are as follows:

ores and concentrates........... 33,240 short tons
smelter products[2].............. 18,920 short tons

These import quotas are the major barriers to zinc imports imposed by the United States. The U.S. Tariff Commission is conducting an investigation to determine whether a sharp rise in imported lead and zinc products—such as zinc sheets and lead litharge—is making ineffective these quotas on primary products.

Nickel ores, nickel oxide and matte are on the free list. The purpose of the duty on refined nickel was to promote smelting and refining in the United States, but it has been too low to furnish any incentive for the construction south of the border of facilities for processing Canadian nickel ores.[3] Under present conditions, it is not an important barrier to trade.

The Canadian nickel industry is understandably concerned about Government subsidies to the Freeport Sulphur Company, which processes Cuban ore. The U.S. Government has invested roughly six million dollars in a plant at Braithwaite, Louisiana, which was sold to Freeport in March 1959 for $236,455.[4] Under a purchase contract, the Government is obligated to buy 271 million pounds of nickel at 75 cents a pound from Freeport Sulphur, and nearly 24 million pounds of by-product cobalt at $2.00 (the current free market price is $1.75). Total domestic production capacity, by 1961, will amount to some 50 million pounds annually from the Freeport Sulphur plant and approximately 20 million pounds from domestic ores. This compares with projected Canadian capacity of around 470 million pounds. Since it

---

1. Lead bullion or base bullion, lead in pigs and bars, lead dross, reclaimed lead, scrap lead, antimonial lead, antimonial scrap lead, type metal, Babbitt metal, solder, all alloys or combinations of lead n.s.p.f.

2. Zinc in blocks, pigs, or slabs, and zinc dust.

3. Bidwell, P., *Raw Materials*, Harper, New York, 1958, page 148.

4. *The Wall Street Journal*, New York, May 12, 1959.

would appear that capacity by that date will be in excess of projected consumption, Canadian exports may be adversely affected to a considerable extent by these subsidies to the U.S. and Cuban industries.

U.S. fluorspar production has, for many years, been greatly exceeded by imports. The major sources of supply are Mexico, Spain, Italy and West Germany. Domestic mines are unable to supply the vastly expanded requirements of U.S. industries, and the Government has resorted to a combination of tariff protection and purchase programs to stimulate output. Thus, while domestic acid-grade fluorspar was quoted in trade journals at about $50 per short ton during 1958, the Government was paying $53 under stockpile contracts; and the industry was further sheltered from foreign competition by a tariff of $2.10.[1]

Although the purchase program has been terminated,[2] survival of the domestic industry is not dependent upon the duty. Its suspension would cause some substitution of imported acid-grade fluorspar for the output of domestic mines owned by the steel and aluminum industries.

A Canadian firm operating fluorspar mines in Newfoundland owns a mill at Wilmington, Delaware, which was constructed with U.S. Government aid. Concentrates processed at this mill from Canadian ore were purchased for the U.S. stockpile under a contract ending in 1957. Following the expiration of this contract, the firm suspended mining operations, as the company was unable to compete in Canadian markets with foreign fluorspar.

The tariff of 1¼ cents per pound on pig aluminum is not highly restrictive under present cost conditions. However, the industry is in a process of rapid change, which could alter the influence of the tariff. U.S. capacity is increasing very rapidly, and expectations are that demand will increase by more than five fold by 1980.[3]

Such a degree of expansion is making necessary a careful reconsideration of power sources, power being the major cost item. One result seems to be a greater utilization of coal and natural gas, and of location near consuming

---

1. Although the metallurgical grade sells for a lower price than the acid grade, the specific tariff is higher ($8.40). This anomaly results from technological progress which has made possible the domestic production of acid-grade concentrates, of which very little were produced in the United States in 1930.

2. The Secretary of the Interior stated that, with the completion of the program in December 1958, the industry "would be oriented at reasonable price and production levels." (Statement of Hon. Fred. A. Seaton, before Senate Interior and Insular Affairs Committee, June 4, 1957). The fluorspar industry has nevertheless petitioned for an investigation by the Office of Civil and Defense Mobilization, on the grounds that imports are threatening to impair the national security. This investigation could result in "adjustment of imports" under the national-security provisions of trade agreements legislation.

3. The projection cited above is from an unpublished manuscript by Mr. Wilbert Fritz, "The Future of Industrial Raw Materials in North America", prepared for The Canadian-American Committee.

centers, so as to offset the higher cost of thermal power by lower transport costs. In addition, greater efficiency in power production is steadily being achieved. New plants in the United States are probably competitive with Canadian, taking into account both location and capital costs.[1] Still, in terms of power potential, Canada retains a natural advantage of various water power sites.

The tariff on semi-fabricated aluminum (plates, sheets, bars and shapes) is effective in excluding Canadian mill products from the U.S. market. Virtually all imports from Canada are in the form of pig aluminum.

Softwood lumber includes spruce, Douglas fir, hemlock, cedar and white pine lumber. Large imports are made from Canada, owing in part to the proximity of the eastern Canadian mills to the northern industrial area of the United States. Quite a number of items, such as logs, wood waste, firewood, sticks, poles, posts, laths, pickets, palings, rails, railroad ties, shingles and shakes are on the free list. Northern white pine lumber is assessed at only 25 cents per thousand feet. For all items, the duty is probably insignificant in relation to labor and transportation costs and selling expenses.

Maple, birch, beech and oak lumber and floorings comprise the bulk of hardwood imports from Canada. The basic rate for hardwood lumber is $1.50 per thousand feet. Beech, birch and maple floorings pay four percent ad valorem. Other hardwood floorings, including oak, are assessed at 16⅔ percent.

Except in the case of oak and other hardwood floorings, these tariffs are probably not significant barriers to imports.

Manufactured Intermediate Products and Consumers' Goods

U.S. tariffs on a number of items of particular interest to Canadian manufacturers are listed in Tables 14 and 15. The dutiable items are classified as to intermediate products and producers' goods, and items used by the ultimate consumer. Although in some cases the estimated ad valorem equivalent can only be indicated in very rough fashion, it is evident that the rates for the two broad categories of manufactured products do not, on the whole, vary significantly from each other. The median rate of 15 to 20 percent in both cases compares with 4 percent for industrial raw materials and fuels, and about 9 percent for agricultural and fish products.[2]

---

1. "Production methods used in the Canadian industry are similar to those employed in the United States and we believe there is little, if any, difference in wages paid or costs of production between the two countries, especially when considering new capacity." (Bruce, Fraser W., President of Alcan Limited, before the Subcommittee on Foreign Trade Policy of the U.S. House Ways and Means Committee, October 31, 1957.)

2. See Table 3.

TABLE 14

U.S. Tariffs on Intermediate Products

Item	Estimated Ad Valorem Equivalent (November 1958)
CHEMICALS	
synthetic phenolic resins	25
cellulose acetate	30
cellophane	$22\frac{1}{2}$[1]
coal tar acids and medicinals	25 to 27
formaldehyde solution	22
glacial acetic acid	15
chlorine	$10\frac{1}{2}$
caustic soda	16
titanium compounds	15[1]
ELECTRICAL EQUIPMENT	
motors	$10\frac{1}{2}$ to $12\frac{1}{2}$[1]
parts of electrical fans and blowers	$17\frac{1}{2}$[1]
generators and miscellaneous heavy equipment	15[1]
TRANSPORTATION EQUIPMENT	
airplanes, aircraft parts and engines	$12\frac{1}{2}$[1]
automobiles and trucks, and parts	$8\frac{1}{2}$ to $10\frac{1}{2}$[1]
TEXTILES	
hose of vegetable fiber	25
asbestos manufactures, except construction materials	$8\frac{1}{2}$ to 10[1]
WOOD PRODUCTS	
plywood	15 to 40
paintbrush handles	$8\frac{1}{2}$[1]
parts for furniture, of wood	$10\frac{1}{2}$[1]
doors, of wood	15[1]
various manufactures of wood	$16\frac{2}{3}$[1]
cigarette paper	60
book and printing paper	8
paperboards	5 to 15
METAL MANUFACTURES	
steel bars, chrome alloyed, over 16¢/lb	$10\frac{1}{2}$[1]
metal cutting tools with excess alloys	30[1]
brass manufactures	19[1]
metal working machines	15[1]
MISCELLANEOUS	
glass bottles, jars and vials	5 to 10

1. Ad valorem rate.

As indicated in Chapter 2, there are some Canadian products of fairly complex manufacture which are exported duty-free to the United States, such as agricultural machinery, typewriters, and items for the defense establishment. However, the bulk of Canadian exports to the United States consists of primary materials (for example metal, fish, and cattle) or manufactures which are essentially semi-processed primary products (newsprint and lumber), rather than manufactured consumers' goods and intermediate products. (See Tables 12 and 13 for examples of the latter.)

As a basis for understanding the current situation, it is interesting to review the effects of Canadian and U.S. commercial policy on the growth

TABLE 15

U.S. Tariffs on Manufactured Consumers' Goods

Item	Estimated Ad Valorem Equivalent (November 1958)
Wool wearing apparel	24 to 41
Earthenware and chinaware	32[1]
Table and artware	67[2]
Aluminum cooking ware, table ware, hollow ware	18 to 22
Linoleum	12½ to 21
Paints and enamels	10½ to 15[3]
Varnishes	8½ to 15[3]
Toys	25 to 90
Tissue papers	11
Writing paper	11 to 20
Jellies, jams, marmalades and fruit butters	8½ to 17½[3]
Whiskey	14
Beer	9
Canned salmon	15[3]
Baked articles (except bread)	8½[3]

1. Average for lower-priced ware. Rockingham earthenware produced in Canada pays 6¼ percent.
2. Average for higher-priced ware.
3. Ad valorem rate.

and development of Canadian industry generally. The U.S. tariff has developed around the principle that U.S. industry should be assisted by making the entry easy for essential raw materials and for products in which the U.S. is deficient, and that entry should be made difficult for manufactures which are competitive with U.S. products. For example, the tariff on aluminum ingot is about 5 percent, while aluminum cooking ware, table ware and hollow ware are charged the ad valorem equivalent of 18 to 22 percent. Analogous contrasts exist between the tariff on copper metal (6 percent) and copper manufactures (7 to 12 percent); raw asbestos (free) and asbestos manufactures (5 to 10½ percent); nickel ore, matte and oxide (free) and nickel semi-fabricated products (12½ to 17½ percent); fresh fish (4 percent) and filleted and frozen blocks (8 percent); and wood products (free to 17 percent, depending on degree of processing and type).

The effects of these and other examples are summarized by Dr. J. Young in the Gordon Commission study, Canadian Commercial Policy, as follows:

In general, the United States tariff, both in terms of rates and customs administration, has provided more favourable treatment for Canadian primary commodities than for goods at a higher stage of manufacture. This differential tariff treatment, to the extent to which it has affected the Canadian economy, has tended to twist Canada's industrial structure away from secondary manufacturing and toward extractive and primary processing industries . . .[1]

1. Young, J. H., *Canadian Commercial Policy*, Royal Commission on Canada's Economic Prospects, 1958, page 147.

A further "twist" in the same direction may have resulted from Canadian tariff policy in recent years. Tariff bargaining by Canada, bilaterally with the United States and later through GATT, has been largely directed at obtaining tariff reductions on raw materials and agricultural foodstuffs, in exchange for granting tariff concessions on manufactured goods. Under the Most-Favoured-Nation principle, Canada does, of course, receive concessions granted on manufactured products to other countries.

Professor Clarence L. Barber has the following to say:

While our Government has on occasion expressed a desire for freer access to the United States market for Canada's manufactured goods, it is difficult to believe that the matter is regarded as urgent. At least it does not merit special trips to Washington by our cabinet ministers as does a threat of quota restrictions on our agricultural exports ... The Government's emphasis on securing favourable tariff treatment and maintaining low costs for our traditional export industries also reflects their belief that these are the industries in which Canada has a comparative advantage whereas our manufacturing industries are protected weaklings to be tolerated but not encouraged.[1]

If, at an early stage of its development, Canadian industry had not been turned inward by both Canadian and U.S. trade barriers, some plants would have been built on a scale large enough to serve the whole North American market. Some Canadian industries would have developed in those locations and along those lines best serving the entire North American market, and would have launched forth to compete throughout the area. By and large, manufacturers have been more concerned about protecting their Canadian markets than about the development of new markets in the United States.

This influence of Canadian and U.S. tariff policy cannot be stressed too strongly. However, another aspect of the problem is often emphasized: that U.S. duties do not allow Canadian manufacturers to expand their plants and secure economies of scale sufficient to enable them to sell in the United States. This is clearly and lucidly presented in the Bank of Nova Scotia *Monthly Review* of October-November, 1953:

The Canadian quarrel with the U.S. tariff is not so much that it keeps out the goods Canada has for sale as that it limits development along natural and economic lines. For instance, side by side with Canada's great specialized lumber, woodpulp and newsprint industries, and using the same raw materials, exist the fine-paper industry, making hundreds of grades of paper for the domestic market, and a host of small wood-product industries. Because they are confined to the home market by the U.S. tariff, the expansion of such smaller industries as these, now that Commonwealth

---

1. Barber, C. L., "Canadian Tariff Policy", *The Canadian Journal of Economics and Political Science*, University of Toronto Press, November 1955, page 528.

markets are almost completely cut off, is virtually limited by the growth of Canadian demand. And, being geared to the needs of a comparatively small market, many of them labor under the disadvantages of small-scale production. Better access to the U.S. market would reduce these handicaps, permitting longer runs and the lower-cost and more efficient production necessary to compete in that market. In time it might lead to increased specialization and the development of other industries as highly economic and fully competitive as Canadian newsprint and woodpulp. But until the broad range of manufactures based on Canadian raw materials attains reasonable and assured access to the U.S. market, progress in this direction is severely handicapped.

In order to know what weight to attach to the factor of scale, it would be necessary to know by how much Canadian costs for a particular product could be reduced from present levels if production were expanded substantially.

Although the scale factor is much too inclusive to be studied in this paper, it does require thoughtful consideration. Many useful insights are provided by the Gordon Commission study, *Canadian Secondary Manufacturing Industry*, which suggests that the key to lower costs of production in Canada is longer production runs; that the problem in many industries is that there are too many firms for the market rather than that the Canadian market is absolutely too small for optimum productive conditions. In this connection, the study mentions specifically the following: producers of relatively standardized machine tools and other metal working machinery; the chemical industry; the fine and specialty paper producers; the textile industry; the iron- and steel-using industries; secondary industries based on the fabrication of resource materials such as aluminum, copper, brass, nickel, asbestos, and petrochemicals; some parts of the clothing industry; and producers of certain types of rubber tires.[1]

Pointing to gains in the relative position of Canadian secondary industry over the past two decades, the authors conclude that certain activities are now almost as efficient as in the United States. These include the brewing and distilling industries, some types of food and fish processing, and some oil-refining operations. However, they add that the effects of smaller-scale and less-specialized operations on the gap which remains between production costs in the two countries "account for not less than three-quarters of this difference."[2]

The authors note that the effects of scale and specialization vary widely: they are probably very substantial in metal fabrication, primary textiles and rubber tires; they are probably slight in more labour-intensive operations,

---

1. Fullerton, D. H., and Hampson, H. A., *Canadian Secondary Manufacturing Industry*, Royal Commission on Canada's Economic Prospects, 1958, pages 88-92.

2. *Ibid.*, pages 92-93.

such as production of clothes and rubber footwear. In addition to the variations among industries, there are also a number of important variations within industries. Although large plants and organizations are known to be common in many spheres of activity, there are usually plants of moderate size in both the United States and Europe that are as efficient as the giants. The relation between scale of production and efficiency has still other dimensions. The pattern of resource use, management practices, and marketing methods throughout the entire economy is of great importance. One must conclude that the "optimum-sized plant" in a given industry in Canada may be quite different from that in the United States, or indeed, from that in Canada itself at different points in time; hence, inter-country size comparisons are not very meaningful. We cannot safely assume that size of operations and productivity are synonymous.

There are a number of factors other than size which make for higher costs in Canada. Among these are higher interest rates, and climatic differences which require heavier construction. More important, perhaps, is the apparent lead of U.S. industry with regard to applied research and technical innovation. Finally, the element of monopoly may be important in some sectors of the Canadian economy.

In addition to the problems involved in projecting cost curves and allowing for the factors of technological change and monopoly, analysis of the U.S. tariff and its effect on Canadian economic development is made difficult by the relation between U.S. firms and their Canadian branches and subsidiaries. In some cases, the Canadian operation may be restrained from competing in the United States because of deliberate company policy. There is, of course, no way to know to what extent this is true, although it is frequently suggested:

"A Canadian firm may be legally free to export to the United States and yet refuse to do so because it is contrary to its policy or 'business ethics'."[1]

In view of the large number of factors involved, and the difficulty of obtaining empirical evidence and documentation, it is difficult to come to any definite conclusions on these controversial matters. The Canadian claim that U.S. tariffs have prevented the development of Canadian industry along natural economic lines is doubtless true. But there is also some truth in the counter-claim that other factors must be invoked to explain the failure of Canada to develop as a major exporter of manufactured goods to the United States. Broad economic reasoning can be invoked to support either position. What is needed above all at this juncture are careful case-by-case studies of the major industry groups which are most strongly affected by trade barriers.

---

1. Plumptre, Wynne, "Exports to the United States", (Quoted in Brecher and Riesman, *Canada-United States Economic Relations*, Royal Commission on Canada's Economic Prospects, 1958, page 180).

Illustrations of these factors are the chemical industry, in which it would appear that Canadian and U.S. tariffs have blocked a natural tendency toward economic integration; the heavy electrical and machine tool industries, in which a number of specialized labour-intensive items are apparently produced in Canada at competitive prices; the manufactured foodstuffs industry, in which substantial U.S. imports from Canada now take place over relatively high tariffs; the wood products industry, in which high U.S. tariffs appear to prevent the further processing in Canada of Canadian forest products; and the automobile industry, in which Canadian specialty items, such as snow blowers and light-tracked vehicles, are now sold over tariffs of 8½ to 12½ percent. In time, a much greater degree of integration might be possible in these and other industries if production were geared to a continental market.

7

Effects of Canadian
Trade Barriers

THE ONLY really meaningful way to assess the restrictiveness of Canadian customs duties is to examine individual industries and commodities. By so doing, one can attempt to get some idea of the extent to which rate reductions would induce additional U.S. imports. Since it is obviously impossible to examine here all of the industries and commodities involved, nine Canadian industries have been selected for special attention. These industries are textiles, primary iron and steel, chemicals, automobiles, industrial machinery, electrical manufactures, paper products, manufactures or iron and steel, and fresh fruits and vegetables. In making this selection, we relied to a large extent on the analysis presented in publications of the Royal Commission on Canada's Economic Prospects, particularly J. H. Young's *Canadian Commercial Policy*. The tariffs which protect these industries may be considered "key" rates, since their removal would do away with the greater part of the tariff protection afforded Canadian producers against competition from the United States.

With the exception of fresh fruits and vegetables, all these key rates are found in secondary manufacturing industries. This is not a coincidence, for this is the sector in which the Canadian producer, frequently confined to a relatively small market, is likely to have higher costs than his U.S. counterpart, and requires protection in order to survive. In their study, *Canadian Secondary Manufacturing Industry*, D. H. Fullerton and H. A. Hampson, conclude, on the basis of evidence submitted by a great many Canadian manufacturers, that the difference in production scale is the basic reason why the American manufacturer can produce more cheaply:

> In summary, in competing with United States producers, Canadian secondary industry is handicapped by its smaller market and inability to obtain the same economies of scale as its American competitors. These economies stem not only from the direct advantages of the large size of market but from greater specialization and concentration of production. (page 78)

The discussion which follows is intended to be strictly preliminary in nature. No effort is made to measure in any exact sense the restrictiveness of particular duties. Needless to say, the conclusions reached are, for the most part, fairly broad generalizations to which one could find many individual exceptions, and if the proper qualifications are not always stated, it springs from a dislike of repetition rather than any unawareness of their need.

Textiles

The greatest source of foreign competition for Canadian cotton and synthetic fabric goods—both primary textiles and manufactured items— is the United States, and any reduction in the tariff would certainly mean substantially greater U.S. imports. This is not true of woolen goods, where the domestic producers' chief competition comes from the United Kingdom.

Most cotton and synthetic fabric imports come from the United States, the proportion ranging between 60 and 80 percent depending on the particular item. These imports include coloured cotton fabrics, unbleached cotton fabrics, a wide variety of cotton clothing, sheets, towels, and many types of synthetic fabrics and clothing. Despite the fact that the U.S. price is significantly below the Canadian price for almost all such items, the Canadian tariff protects a large domestic industry which currently supplies about 40 percent of the cotton-fabric market, 70 percent of the primary synthetic-fabric market, and 90 percent of the clothing market. The duties for most textile products are quite high, as the following table indicates (although there are also some lower duties, such as the 7½ percent rate on synthetic staple):

TABLE 16

Canadian Tariff Rates on Selected
Cotton and Synthetic Fabric Goods

Item	MFN Rate	Ad Valorem Equivalent (Percent)	BP Rate (Percent)
Cotton yarn....................	17½% + 3¢/lb.	20	15
Cotton fabrics..................	15% + 3¢/lb.	19.5	15
Bleached cotton fabrics..........	17½% + 3¢/lb.	20	17½
Printed cotton fabrics over 80¢/lb...	17½% + 3¢/lb.	20	17½
Cotton clothing.................	25%	—	25
Except tablecloths, sheets, etc......	22½%	—	22½
Synthetic yarns.................	22½%	—	Various
Synthetic fabrics...............	25% + 30¢/lb.	38.5	22½
Synthetic textile clothing..........	27½%	—	20

Source: The Canadian Tariff. The item descriptions are abbreviated and the ad valorem equivalents approximations only. Both are those found in Young's *Canadian Commercial Policy*, Table 9, pages 114-117.

The MFN ad valorem equivalent rates on cotton yarn and fabrics run around 20 percent; on cotton clothing, 25 percent; on synthetic yarns, 22½ percent; on synthetic fabrics, 38½ percent; and on synthetic textile clothing, 27½ percent. The domestic industry takes full advantage of these rates and is, in fact, heavily dependent on them. During the last 15 years, with the ad valorem equivalents of the numerous specific textile rates declining due to price inflation and with foreign competition becoming keener, the industry has come under increasing pressure as profits and wages have failed to keep pace with those of Canadian industry generally.

Primary Iron and Steel

Up to the rolling-mill level—that is, for iron ore, pig iron, and iron and steel ingots—the Canadian tariff is not an important factor in restricting imports from the United States. Iron ore is allowed free entry into Canada, and imports from the United States are sizeable, amounting to $37 million in 1956; exports to the United States, however, are much greater ($114 million in 1956). Canadian producers of pig iron, and iron and steel ingots are competitive with U.S. producers, the tariff rates are relatively low, and imports from the United States are very small. In 1956, exports of pigs, ingots, blooms and billets to the United States amounted to $24 million.

At the rolling-mill level, however, Canadian costs become somewhat higher than costs in the United States because of the less-specialized nature of Canadian output, and the tariff restricts U.S. competition in a long list of products. The severity of this restriction, of course, varies from one type of product to another, and also varies from one section of Canada to another. Before examining this question further, let us look at some of the prevailing tariff rates:

TABLE 17

Canadian Tariff Rates on Selected Primary Steel Products

Item	MFN Rate (Percent)	BP Rate (Percent)
Semi-finished iron or steel (blooms, billets, slabs or sheet bars)	5	Free
Hot-rolled bars or rods	10	5
Angles, beams, etc., n.o.p.	10	5
Wide-flange beams	$5 per ton	Free
Hot- or cold-rolled plate	10	5
Flanged or disked plate	20	5
Plate, n.o.p.	15	5
Hot-rolled sheet or strip	10	5
Cold-rolled sheet or strip	15	5
Sheet or strip coated with lead or an alloy of lead and tin	Free	Free
Rough castings, n.o.p.	20	15
Forgings, n.o.p.	22½	17½
Pipes and tubes, n.o.p.	20	12½
Cold-drawn pipes and tubes	5	Free
Wire, n.o.p.	20	15

Note: The item descriptions are abbreviated in most cases.
Source: The Canadian Tariff.

As the table indicates, the rates are concentrated around the 10-percent level for rolling-mill products, which is low compared to many other rates protecting Canadian secondary industries. In addition, many items enter free or at reduced rates, or are eligible for drawbacks, provided they are for certain specific end uses. For example, all steel for shipbuilding and the manufacture of agricultural implements and tractor engines is duty-free, and the duty on skelp, plate, sheet and strip is reduced to MFN 7½ percent when imported for use in the manufacture of pipes or tubes.

The rates, however, need not be any higher to provide protection for the domestic industry. The cost advantage of U.S. mills is not very large, and the Canadian mills enjoy a considerable freight advantage in the big Ontario and Quebec markets. In fact, the freight advantage is, in many cases, a more important barrier to U.S. imports than the tariff, and frequently in the central Canadian market is so important that the tariff tends to represent a purely nominal trade barrier. In other words, even if the steel tariffs were removed, the U.S. mills could not compete with many products of the Hamilton companies (Steel Company of Canada and Dominion Foundries and Steel) because their laid-down costs, at least in the Toronto area would still be higher, since their basic price advantage would be more than offset by their freight disadvantage. However, with respect to a great many other steel items, U.S. mills are competitive in the central Canadian markets—sometimes due to their readiness to absorb part of their freight disadvantage—and any reduction in tariff duties would most certainly mean additional imports.

The fact that U.S. mills are competitive in the Canadian market becomes obvious when one realizes that imports supply between 25 and 30 percent of the rolling-mill products market, with about 75 percent of imports coming from the United States. The most important items are structurals and un-coated sheet and strip. Not all of these imports, however, compete with domestic production. Many large items, such as wide-flange structural sections, sheets wider than 52 inches, plates wider than 100 inches, are not produced in Canada at all, or only to a very limited extent, and in such cases, the tariff is not a significant barrier. The same is true of terneplate and many specialty items.

In contrast with their position in the central Canadian market, domestic Canadian steel mills are at a freight disadvantage to many U.S. mills in the western Canadian market. While Algoma Steel at Sault Ste. Marie is the most westerly of all the major Canadian mills, there are big American producers in Utah, Colorado, California and Washington. For this reason, British Columbia and the Prairie provinces import a much higher proportion of their steel requirements than the other provinces, and the tariff rates appear to have more restrictive effects.

Finally, Canadian mills are facing increasing competition from overseas producers in the west coast and Montreal markets, although the proportion of overseas imports is still relatively small. Steel mills in the United Kingdom,

Germany and other parts of western Europe, as well as in Japan, are becoming more competitive, and are taking advantage of low ocean freight costs to ship their wares to Canada. The recent opening of the St. Lawrence Seaway may extend their area of operations deeper into central and western Canada. Therefore, the trade barriers against steel imports on a Most-Favoured-Nation basis affect not only U.S. mills, but also those of many overseas countries.

Chemicals

The chemical industry in Canada, like most other secondary industries, faces its keenest competition from U.S. manufacturers. The highly capital-intensive procedures in the industry mean that the smaller output and lower degree of specialization result in higher production costs than in the United States. One finds, therefore, that even in cases of tariff protection of 15 to 25 percent on dutiable items, Canada imports large amounts of chemical products from American sources. In 1955, total chemical imports ($300 million) amounted to about one-quarter of total Canadian consumption, and 85 percent of these imports came from the United States. Here are just a few of the rates on chemical products:

TABLE 18

Canadian Tariff Rates on Selected Chemical Products

Item	MFN Rate	Ad Valorem Equivalent	BP Rate
Chemicals and drugs, n.o.p., of a kind not produced in Canada	15%	—	Free
Ethylene glycol	10%	—	10%
Nitrate of ammonia, n.o.p.	25%	—	Free
Acids, n.o.p., of a kind not produced in Canada	15%	—	Free
Chemical compounds and preparations	25%	—	25%
Toilet soap, n.o.p.	22½%	—	15%
Soap powders, n.o.p.	20%	—	15%
Cosmetics	22½%	—	15%
Paints, per gallon	85¢	20%	75¢
Varnishes, lacquers, etc.	15% ⎫	— ⎫	5% ⎫
and per gallon	15¢ ⎭	20% ⎭	15¢ ⎭
Fertilizers, manufactured, n.o.p.	5%	—	Free
Synthetic resins—various	Free—7½%	—	Free—7½%
Synthetic resins, n.o.p.	15%	—	15%
Manufactures of synthetic resins, n.o.p.	20%	—	15%

Note: The item descriptions are abbreviated.
Source: The Canadian Tariff.

About 40 percent of Canada's requirements for heavy organic chemicals is imported from the United States. One reason for this high figure is the fact that Canadian manufacturers do not as yet produce a complete range of goods. To the extent that U.S. goods are not competing with a domestic product, a tariff reduction would have little effect on the volume of imports. Canada also imports a major proportion of her primary plastic requirements from the United States, where the industry is 30 times larger. Despite higher costs, however, and despite a polyetheline tariff of only 7½ percent, Canada has developed a relatively big plastics industry.

Canada is more self-sufficient in consumer chemical products than in industrial chemicals, importing about 10 to 15 percent of her requirements. Canadian firms manufacture a very wide range of products. With respect to paints, varnishes and lacquers, Canadian costs are similar to those in the United States, owing to the relatively small optimum size of plant, and imports amount to only about 5 percent of domestic requirements.

Canada is not so competitive in drugs and pharmaceuticals, and imports amount to one-quarter of the home market. The high tariff on soaps and soap powders similarly restricts imports from the United States to a very low level, despite (except for toilet soap) more economic production there.

The most notable exception to the normal cost relationship between Canadian and U.S. manufacturers is in the production of certain primary chemicals, such as heavy industrial inorganics (chlorine, sulphuric acid, etc.), and fertilizers. These products enjoy a relatively large domestic or export market, being used extensively by the natural resource or farming industries, and Canadian costs are very competitive on world markets. Although the actual rates on heavy industrial inorganics are no lower than most chemical rates, the effective protection given domestic producers is quite small, since most buyers are exporters and, as such, are frequently entitled to duty drawbacks of 99 percent. In the case of fertilizers, the primary rate of duty is only 5 percent.

Although Canada is a major exporter of fertilizer to the United States and to other parts of the world, she imports a large part of her heavy inorganics (about 40 percent of the home market) from U.S. companies. The principal reason is that high transportation costs for these bulky, low unit cost commodities make it difficult for Canadian manufacturers in Ontario and Quebec to meet the laid-down price of Oregon, Washington, and California firms in the western Canada market.

The chemical industry, unlike textiles and primary iron and steel, is owned or controlled chiefly by U.S. parent corporations such as Monsanto, Dow, and Du Pont. These corporations have tremendous capital investments in Canadian plants and equipment, and the present pattern of production clearly reflects trade barriers on both sides of the border. As already noted above, these barriers have been sufficiently important to prevent the development of an economically-integrated chemical industry in North America.

Automobiles

Due to the complex nature of automobile production and the large capital investment required, the economies of mass production and specialization are extremely important. This is particularly true when one considers that model changes requiring new dies and tooling occur now as frequently as once a year. Since Canadian output is approximately one-twentieth of American output, it is not surprising that Canadian manufacturing costs are considerably higher than those in the United States. Therefore, although the Canadian industry is quite efficient for its size, the cost of producing a typical lower-priced automobile in Canada appears to be about 10 to 15 percent greater than in the United States. This cost disadvantage applies not only to the assembly-line stage of production, but also to the manufacture of component parts, where Canadian parts manufacturers can approach U.S. costs only on simpler, large-volume items. With respect to convertibles and higher-priced automobiles, such as Cadillacs, Lincolns, and Chryslers, the small demand in Canada means that the cost of domestic production is prohibitive; these vehicles are therefore imported by Canadian manufacturers from their respective parent companies in the United States.

Obviously, the Canadian automotive industry could not have developed to its present state had it not been for substantial tariff protection from U.S. competition. The important rates are shown in the following table:

TABLE 19

Canadian Tariff Rates on Selected Automotive Items

Item	MFN Rate (Percent)	BP Rate (Percent)
Automobiles, trucks and buses...................	17½	Free
List of automobile parts:		
(i) if not made in Canada.....................	Free	Free
(ii) if made in Canada.......................	17½	Free
List of automobile parts, if not made in Canada, and the required Commonwealth content achieved.....	Free	Free
Parts, n.o.p.......................................	25	Free
Used or secondhand automobiles.................	Prohibited from entry	

Note: The descriptions of tariff items are in abbreviated form.
Source: The Canadian Tariff.

Already mentioned in the discussion of classification problems, is the necessity for Canadian automobile manufacturers to achieve a certain Commonwealth (in effect, Canadian) content in their production costs in order to import free-of-duty all parts listed under tariff item 438c. For manufacturers who achieve an output of over 20,000 automobiles per year, this requirement is 60 percent, falling to 40 percent for those with an output of under 10,000. The requirement for the major producers (General Motors, Ford, and Chrysler) is 60 percent, although certain model lines have recently come close to this limit. In this way, then, the tariff encourages the production of parts in Canada, but at the same time provides some flexibility for the manufacturer with respect to whether he buys in the domestic or U.S. market. In addition, the parts industry is protected by a tariff of either 17½ or 25 percent on items made in Canada, with most falling in the latter category.

As Table 17 shows, the tariff rate on new automobiles coming in from the United States is 17½ percent. This rate is high enough to restrict almost completely the importation of U.S. cars, except the higher-priced models. To some extent, however, this lack of U.S. competition is also due to the close corporate relationship between Canadian and U.S. manufacturers. It would not be reasonable, for example, for a parent company in the United States to export to Canada and market in competition with its subsidiary.

The net effect of the Canadian automobile tariff schedule has been to restrict imports of U.S. cars to a level representing less than 10 percent of the Canadian market, and automobile parts to between 40 and 50 percent of the Canadian market.

Although one can safely assume that, had there never been Canadian duties on automobiles and parts, the great bulk of the Canadian market would have been supplied by imports from the United States, it is not as easy to assess the present restrictiveness of these duties.

Industrial Machinery

The greatest proportion of industrial machinery comes into Canada under one of the twin tariff items 427 or 427a. Item 427 covers machinery and machinery parts n.o.p., of a type made in Canada, and provides rates of MFN 22½ percent, BP 10 percent; item 427a covers machinery and parts n.o.p., of a class or kind not made in Canada, and provides lower rates of MFN 7½ percent, BP Free. In addition, there are a large number of "end-use" items under which certain industrial machinery to be used for a specific purpose in Canada is admitted at low rates or free of duty. These "end-use" items in most cases apply to machinery for use in the extractive industries.

Despite these protective duties, Canada satisfies an exceptionally high percentage of her requirements from foreign sources, chiefly from the United States. In recent years, in fact, 60 to 70 percent of the Canadian market has been supplied by foreign producers, with about 85 percent of imports originating in the United States. The bulk of these imports from the United States represent relatively standardized products—such as machine tools and other metal-working machinery, textile and printing machinery—where the import share of the domestic market amounts to nearly 100 percent in many cases. In the production of this type of equipment, the advantages of scale are extremely large, and even with tariff protection, the Canadian manufacturer's costs are usually too high to compete with his U.S. counterpart. What domestic production there is consists mostly of assembling, complex parts being acquired from the parent or associate company in the United States.

On the other hand, custom machinery is normally labour-intensive, and long runs are not an important cost consideration. Here, Canada supplies a much larger proportion of the home market, the import share running as low as 35 percent for pulp and paper machinery; and even down to 6 percent for water wheels and turbines, where construction must take place largely on the site. The principal competition is not from the United States but from low-wage overseas countries, especially the United Kingdom. The low BP rate is, of course, a great help to U.K. manufacturers with respect to U.S. competition. Canadian manufacturers, however, have considerable natural protection when it comes to the type of items involving custom work, as well as certain more standardized items, and may frequently make sales despite lower prices submitted by foreign producers. A certain amount of natural protection results from their proximity to the customer, enabling closer consultation prior to the purchase, earlier deliveries, and better future servicing in many instances. Canadian producers are also more experienced in building specialized machinery for use in the primary industries.

Present tariff duties do not appear to have any substantial restrictive effects upon many standardized items from the United States, such as textile machinery and machine tools, since U.S. producers already supply a very large proportion of the total market. Table 20 lists the import share of the domestic market—comprising imports from all countries—for the various categories of industrial machinery:

TABLE 20

**Import Share of the Canadian Market
for Industrial Machinery, 1954**

Type of Machinery	Total Domestic Market (Thousands of Dollars)	Import Share (Percent)
Printing and publishing machinery..................	23,936	98.0
Textile machinery................................	11,706	98.0
Metal-working machinery..........................	63,713	85.8
Industrial engines................................	47,936	73.2
Mining, metallurgical and oil well machinery.........	80,721	71.7
Construction equipment...........................	26,508	70.5
Woodworking machinery..........................	8,647	64.9
Logging and sawmill machinery....................	17,404	60.9
Food-processing machinery........................	17,094	59.3
Air compressors.................................	13,163	53.7
Materials-handling equipment.....................	64,145	38.5
Pulp and paper machinery........................	20,778	35.9
Power pumps...................................	27,198	34.6
Water wheels and turbines........................	16,543	6.2
Other machinery................................	162,441	75.9
Total...	601,933	66.6

Source: Urwick, Currie Limited, *The Canadian Industrial Machinery Industry*, Royal Commission on Canada's Economic Prospects, February 1956, page 27.

Cases in which existing trade barriers appear to have significant restrictive effects upon potential U.S. suppliers include certain types of materials-handling equipment, construction equipment, and food-processing machinery.

Electrical Manufactures

At the present time, Canada imports approximately one-quarter of her requirements of electrical goods. Between 85 and 90 percent of these goods come from the United States, another 10 percent from the United Kingdom, and the rest from other countries like Switzerland and Sweden. Most products carry an MFN rate of 20 or 22½ percent and a BP rate of 15 or 18 percent.

In assessing the restrictiveness of these duties on U.S. imports, it is convenient to divide electrical manufactures into three broad categories, as outlined by Mr. C. L. Barber in his study, *The Canadian Electrical Manufacturing Industry* (September 1956) for the Royal Commission on Canada's Economic Prospects.

First, there is a group of products which are largely custom-built, such as large waterwheel generators, large power transformers, power cable, heavy switchgear and some types of telephone and telegraph apparatus. The labour content is relatively high for this type of equipment, the optimum size of plant is fairly small, and Canadian costs are in line with U.S. costs. Foreign competition is stronger from low-wage overseas countries than from the United States. About 15 percent of the industry's total output falls into this first group.

At the other extreme are standard, mass-produced goods, where the Canadian market is sufficiently large to maintain a production unit close to the optimum size, thereby enabling Canadian costs to be competitive with those of U.S. manufacturers. In this category are products such as light bulbs, cheaper conventional washing machines, floor polishers, cord sets, some types of lighting fixtures, and small heating appliances. For this group and the first group mentioned above, U.S. imports tend to be much smaller than the industrial average.

Within these two extremes, however, is the most important class of electrical products, accounting for perhaps 80 percent of the industry's market. For these products, the optimum size of plant is large, the Canadian market is limited, and Canadian costs tend to be higher than in the United States. In most cases, the cost relationship is such that a substantial domestic industry can survive with tariff protection, but large quantities of goods still come in from the United States over the tariff. Typical of these products are electrical ranges and refrigerators (including components), which Barber estimates are 20 and 17 percent higher in price, respectively, in Canada than in the United States.

The higher costs are due to many factors: the use of multi-purpose rather than special purpose machinery, more time spent in changeovers, less automatic machinery and more expensive design, tooling and process engineering costs per unit—all of which are related to shorter production runs. Commenting on evidence presented by J. H. Goss, President, Canadian General

Electric, concerning the optimum size of plant for the production of refrigerators and ranges, Barber says, "If an optimum production unit can produce upwards of 500,000 units it is evident that a single plant for each product could produce all of Canada's requirements for electric ranges and refrigerators and not be employed full-time" (page 47). In 1955, 34 percent of the domestic market for refrigerators and cookstoves was supplied by imports, almost all from the United States. Obviously the tariff has important restrictive effects.

On the other hand, the cost differential for some items in this last category is considerably lower than the existing tariff protection. In such cases, the import share of the domestic market is normally smaller, and a greater tariff reduction would be required to induce a given increment in imports. For some of these products, such as lamps and certain larger-volume small appliances, the cost disadvantage of Canadian manufacturers is relatively small. For others, the effective protection given by the tariff is quite high— higher than the nominal tariff rate which applies. For example, the duty on wire and cable is 20 percent, but since the cost of raw materials may account for perhaps 60 percent of the finished products' value, and because this raw material is about the same price in Canada as the United States, the manufacturing costs can be up to 50 percent greater in Canada and still enable producers to compete with U.S. manufacturers. In addition to wire and cable, this group of products would include batteries, certain lamps, and radio tubes.

Finally, there are, in this third category, many items where production costs in Canada are prohibitive and, even with tariff protection, little or no manufacture takes place in Canada. For example, many types of instruments and meters, generators, industrial control equipment, and welding apparatus are not produced in Canada, the U.S. imports supplying the whole of the Canadian market. Obviously, the tariff is not a real barrier to such imports.

In the related electronics industry, conditions are similar—that is, for many products the limited Canadian market means higher costs and dependence on tariff protection of around 20 percent. One notable exception is television picture tubes, which apparently can be produced as cheaply in Canada as in the United States, due in part to the free importation of the expensive glass envelopes for these tubes from the United States. Fullerton and Hampson, in their Royal Commission study, point out that there are other factors besides the tariff which protect the electronics industry:

> In appraising the position of the Canadian electronics industry, it must be noted that the extent of its tariff protection, around 20%, is increased by several special administrative and legislative procedures. Between one-quarter and one-third of the industry's output in recent years has been purchased by the government for its defence programme; in many cases government purchases are made not solely on cost considerations and are designed to encourage Canadian production. We have already referred to

the requirements of the Canadian Standards Association; these may make modifications of some foreign designs necessary, and thus raise the costs of the foreign product, and possibly prohibit its entry into Canada. In addition, the operations of Canadian Radio Patents Limited, set up to pool patents and to facilitate licensing negotiations and royalty payments procedures for most electronic products, has some protective effect. (page 88)

Paper Products

Included in this group of products are: book, writing and groundwood papers; paperboard; wrapping papers; and tissue, sanitary and specialty papers. Unlike newsprint and market pulp, which Canada exports to the United States in large quantities free of duty, paper products are limited to the domestic market because of U.S. tariffs. This, in turn, means that the Canadian manufacturers' costs are considerably higher than in the United States because of smaller production runs and related disadvantages. Despite the lower price of U.S. products, however, imports are severely restricted by the Canadian tariff, which provides for MFN rates of 20 to 25 percent: paper of all kinds, 22½ percent; all manufactures of paper, 25 percent; and paperboard containers, 20 percent. The result is that the import share of the market is less than 5 percent.

Manufactures of Iron and Steel

Basket item 446a of the Canadian tariff provides rates of BP 10 percent, MFN 22½ percent for all those manufactures of iron and steel which are not provided for elsewhere in the schedule. A large volume of goods enter Canada from the United States under this item, and there is no doubt that the tariff does limit imports of many commodities in this category.

Fresh Fruits and Vegetables

Most fresh fruits and vegetables are covered by an ad valorem tariff rate of 10 percent and, in addition, an alternative specific rate of 1 to 3¼ cents per pound. The specific rate can be applied for a certain number of weeks during the year, and is designed to give greater protection against U.S. competition during the peak Canadian marketing season. In many instances, climatic differences mean that the peak production period in the United States precedes that in Canada and, without additional protection, the Canadian market would be flooded with U.S. produce when domestic producers are coming to the market. The specific duty, through its regressiveness, provides extra protection against low prices.

The domestic producer has frequently been troubled by cheap end-of-season fresh fruits and vegetables coming on to the market from the United

94

States at the height of the Canadian season. In 1958, the Customs Act was amended to allow a means of restricting such foreign competition. When the market price in the export country has declined as a result of the advanced season or marketing period to a level which, in the opinion of the Minister of National Revenue, does not represent a normal price, the value shall be the average value of importations during the preceding three years. This, of course, makes it possible to levy dumping duties on cheap produce from U.S. growers.

There are a few fresh fruits and vegetables which enter Canada free of duty or at exceptionally low rates. Usually this applies to produce not grown in Canada on a commercial basis, such as oranges, grapefruit and lemons. In the case of potatoes and apples, however, the low rates are due to the strong competitive position of domestic producers vis-a-vis U.S. producers. The great bulk of Canada's imports of fresh fruits and vegetables consists of citrus fruits and other products which cannot be grown in Canada for climatic reasons. In addition, many other imports enter at times of the year when the produce is not in season domestically. It would seem, then, that the existing trade barriers are successful in restricting most U.S. imports at times when they would seriously compete with domestic producers.

Canadian-American Committee Members

Co-chairmen

R. DOUGLAS STUART
Chairman of the Board, The Quaker Oats Company, Chicago, Ill.

ROBERT M. FOWLER
President, Canadian Pulp & Paper Association, Montreal, Que.

Members

ARTHUR S. ADAMS
President, American Council on Education, Washington, D. C.
WILLIAM L. BATT
Philadelphia, Penna.
RALPH P. BELL
Vice-President, Bank of Nova Scotia, Halifax, Nova Scotia
L. J. BELNAP
Chairman, Consolidated Paper Corporation Limited, Montreal, Que.
HAROLD BOESCHENSTEIN
President, Owens-Corning Fiberglas Corporation, Toledo, Ohio
J. E. BROWNLEE
President, United Grain Growers Limited, Calgary, Alta.
L. S. BUCKMASTER
General President, United Rubber, Cork, Linoleum and Plastic Workers of America, AFL-CIO, Akron, Ohio
GEORGE BURT
Director, Region No. 7, United Automobile, Aircraft & Agricultural Implement Workers of America, AFL-CIO-CLC, Windsor, Ont.
BROOKE CLAXTON
Vice-President and General Manager, Metropolitan Life Insurance Company, Ottawa, Ont.
A. HOLLIS EDENS
President, Duke University, Durham, N. C.
MARCEL FARIBAULT
President and General Manager, General Trust of Canada, Montreal, Que.
HAROLD S. FOLEY
Vice-Chairman of the Board, MacMillan, Bloedel and Powell River Company Limited, Vancouver, B.C.
CLINTON S. GOLDEN
Solebury, Bucks County, Penna.
DONALD GORDON
Chairman and President, Canadian National Railways, Montreal, Que.
W. L. GORDON
President, J. D. Woods & Gordon Limited, Toronto, Ont.
H. H. HANNAM
President, Canadian Federation of Agriculture, Ottawa, Ont.
F. PEAVEY HEFFELFINGER
Chairman of the Board, F. H. Peavey & Company, Minneapolis, Minn.
JAMES H. HILTON
President, Iowa State College, Ames, Ia.
STANLEY C. HOPE
President, SoundScriber Corporation, New York, N. Y.
T. V. HOUSER
Director, Sears, Roebuck & Co., Chicago, Ill.
CHARLES L. HUSTON, JR.
President, Lukens Steel Company, Coatesville, Penna.
FRANK W. JENKS
President, International Harvester Company Chicago, Ill.
CLAUDE JODOIN
President, Canadian Labour Congress, Ottawa, Ont.
W. S. KIRKPATRICK
President, The Consolidated Mining and Smelting Company, Montreal, Que.

J. H. MOWBRAY JONES
President, Bowaters Mersey Paper Co. Ltd., Liverpool Nova Scotia.
JOSEPH D. KEENAN
International Secretary, International Brotherhood of Electrical Workers, AFL-CIO, Washington, D. C.
R. A. LAIDLAW
Secretary and Director, R. Laidlaw Lumber Company, Limited, Toronto, Ont.
MAURICE LAMONTAGNE
Ottawa, Ont.
E. H. LANE
Chairman and Director, The Lane Company, Inc., Altavista, Va.
HERBERT H. LANK
President, DuPont Company of Canada Limited, Montreal, Que.
DONALD MacDONALD
Secretary-Treasurer, Canadian Labour Congress, Ottawa, Ont.
N. A. M. MacKENZIE
President, The University of British Columbia, Vancouver, B. C.
W. A. MACKINTOSH
Vice Chancellor and Principal, Queen's University, Kingston, Ont.
JAMES L. MADDEN
Vice-President, Scott Paper Company, Chester, Penna.
WILLIAM MAHONEY
National Director, United Steelworkers of America, AFL-CIO-CLC, Toronto, Ont.
JEAN MARCHAND
General Secretary, The Canadian and Catholic Confederation of Labour, Quebec City, Que.
JAMES A. McCONNELL
Ithaca, N. Y.
J. MORRIS
President, District Council No. 1, International Woodworkers of America, AFL-CIO-CLC, Vancouver, B. C.
HERSCHEL D. NEWSOM
Master, National Grange, Washington, D. C
CHARLES A. PERLITZ, JR.
Executive Vice-President, Continental Oil Company, Houston, Tex.
R. E. POWELL
Honorary Chairman, Aluminum Company of Canada, Ltd., Montreal, Que.
HERBERT V. PROCHNOW
Vice-President, The First National Bank of Chicago, Chicago, Ill.
MICHAEL ROSS
Director, Department of International Affairs, AFL-CIO, Washington, D. C.
RHYS M. SALE
President, Ford Motor Company of Canada, Limited, Toronto, Ont.
GEORGE P. SCHOLLIE
General Vice-President, International Association of Machinists, Montreal, Que.
H. CHRISTIAN SONNE
President, South Ridge Corporation, New York, N. Y.
ALLAN SPROUL
Kentfield, Calif.